# Last Person Rural

OTHER BOOKS BY NOEL PERRIN

*A Passport Secretly Green*

*Dr. Bowdler's Legacy:*
*A History of Expurgated Books*

*Amateur Sugar Maker*

*Vermont in All Weathers*

*The Adventures of Jonathan Corncob*
*Loyal American Refugee*
*Written by Himself (Editor)*

*First Person Rural:*
*Essays of a Sometime Farmer*

*Second Person Rural:*
*More Essays of a Sometime Farmer*

*Third Person Rural:*
*Further Essays of a Sometime Farmer*

*Giving Up the Gun:*
*Japan's Reversion to the Sword, 1543–1879*

*A Reader's Delight*

*A Noel Perrin Sampler*

# LAST
# PERSON
# RURAL

ESSAYS BY

## NOEL PERRIN

*illustrations by Michael McCurdy*

DAVID R. GODINE, PUBLISHER ∾ BOSTON

First published in 1991 by
David R. Godine, Publisher, Inc.
*Horticultural Hall*
300 Massachusetts Avenue
Boston, Massachusetts 02115

Library of Congress Cataloging-in-Publication Data
Perrin, Noel.
Last person rural : essays / by Noel Perrin. — 1st ed.
p.      cm.
ISBN 0-87923-914-X (alk. paper)
1. Country life—Vermont—Anecdotes.
2. Vermont—Anecdotes. 3. Perrin, Noel. I. Title.
S521.5.V5P48 1991
974.3'63—dc20        91-55520   CIP

ACKNOWLEDGMENTS: *"Dawn Walking" is reprinted by permission of* Walking
Magazine. *"In Praise of Old Equipment," "Hands Across the Pasture," "War on the
Farm," and "The Lesson of the Bolt Weevils" are reprinted by permission of* Harrowsmith. *"Gardeners' Glut" is reprinted by permission of* Mother Earth. *"Smooth
Operators" is reprinted by permission of* Vermont Magazine. *"Farmers' TV," and "Old
MacDonald Lost His Farm" are reprinted by permission of* TV Guide. *"A Vermont
Christmas" is reprinted by permission of* Land's End, Inc. *"A Lesson From the Cows" is
reprinted by permission of* Readers Digest. *"778 Prizes for Sheep" is reprinted by
permission of* Smithsonian. *"Joyful Stones" and "Cows and Pleasure" are reprinted by
permission of* Vermont Life. *"Mulcho Man" and "Gardeners and Their Books" are
reprinted by permission of the* New York Times. *"Tough Old Men" is reprinted by
permission of* Yankee. *"Baling the Village" is reprinted by permission of* New England
Monthly. *"Why I Still (Blush) Heat with Wood," "A Pond of One's Own," "A Truck
With Pull," "The Woodlot Adviser," "A Crop From the Coppice," "The One-eyed Witch
of Thetford," "The Price is Wrong," "Raining Limes and Lemons" and "My Farm Is Safe
Forever" are reprinted by permission of* Country Journal. *"The Body of New England"
is reprinted by permission of* Ambassador, *"Death of a Farmer" is reprinted by
permission of the* San Jose Mercury-News. *All appear here in slightly revised form.*

FIRST EDITION
*Printed in the United States of America*

*For Anne, with whom it is joy
to share a book, two farms, a life.*

# Foreword

∾

ONE OF THE PROBLEMS all writers face is dealing with their own past work. They are very apt to say things in print, quite sincerely meaning them, and then later to change their minds. This makes them feel foolish.

Eight years ago, when I published *Third Person Rural*, I said it would be the last book of country essays I'd ever write. And I meant it. For one thing, I'd run out of grammar. For another, I thought I would be doing fewer country things in the future, and in particular less farming. I was a settled divorced person at the time, and my children were nearly grown. Farming is perfectly possible for a single person, but it is not nearly so joyous as for a family. It's not nearly so practical, either.

Thoreau seemed happy enough, planting, growing, and harvesting his beans all by himself—but then, he was raising a cash crop, to prove a thesis. (Thesis: that he or anyone could pick up a year's pocket money in one summer by an "honest and agreeable method." He almost proved it, but not quite. He had hoped to make $10. From his two acres of beans and potatoes he netted $8.71. Of course, roast beef was then 3 cents a pound, and a haircut cost a dime.)

Furthermore, Thoreau did not really live solitary. He walked the scant mile into town several times a week to have dinner with his parents, or with the Emersons. If he had stayed home and done subsistence farming, he would have found it highly desirable to have a family. That is, people to raise beans for and discuss bean culture with, and maybe even to help with the hoeing. Properly done, farming is a social activity, one of the oldest and one of the best. And a farm family remains one of the very few truly functional units in modern America.

What I couldn't know eight years ago was that I would get married again—and to a woman who is the same kind of country person that I am myself. That is, an eager convert. She had nothing to do with keeping chickens or raising sheep when she was a child. In her twenties, she lived in Paris. Now she is harder to pry loose from our two farms than I am. A one-day trip to Boston, and you'd think she was never going to see the horses or pigs or chickens again.

An extra rural bonus: She has a fourteen-year-old son with a good appetite. He won't touch home-grown pork, but in the intervals of McDonald's he is a wonderful consumer of our organic salad stuff, Silver Queen corn, etc. So are our various daughters when they get home. I am back farming full tilt.

Eight years ago I also said that though I planned no more rural books, I did still have a few rustic essays in mind, in particular one on fence posts. At that time I was halfway through a ten-year test of every kind of tree that grows on this place, to see which ones would last longest as farm posts. The test is long over now, and the clear winner was red oak. I did write the article. But it turned out to be boring, even to me. It will never be published; instead it joins the slag heap that every writer possesses. Mine contains four abortive books, a dozen fully written but failed articles, and at least thirty that I started and had the good sense not to finish. There are also a small number of short stories, written in my twenties and so bad that it takes real courage to admit to their existence.

What's left to go here? Four different kinds of essays, maybe five.

The first kind, which I've been writing for many years, is concerned with the practicalities of life in the country: buying equipment, figuring out what to do with an old barn if you're not a farmer, making a little pond. The second is about the impracticalities of life in the country: taking walks with children, building stone walls more for looks than use, looking at frosted trees.

The third is the kind of essay one might write from a beleaguered city—only I happen to be writing from a beleaguered countryside. Something there is that doesn't love a New England farm, and that something is called a developer. Or, rather, the developer loves them dearly, but his embrace is death.

And then there are several somethings that don't love countryside anywhere. Heavy industry is one of them. It has poisoned much of the planet, including many places you wouldn't expect. My own little Vermont, the most rural state in the East, is also among five states in the Union with the most badly polluted air. The rain is killing our maples. The snow comes down already acid.

We don't make that polluted air ourselves; we get it in a steady stream, night and day, from coal-fired power plants a thousand miles away. If we were smart, we would pick up our Green Mountains and our little valleys, our cornfields and pastures, and move somewhere where the air would come to us from across a wide ocean. No one has figured out how to pollute sea air yet.

Another hater of countryside is that mysterious something called progress. With one finger of one hand, progress puts a four-lane highway through a secluded valley. Then with that same finger it shoves a seven-hundred-mile powerline across some of the best farmland in South Dakota and Minnesota, a huge high-voltage line that just may bring cancer with it. With another finger, progress begins to turn out artificial cotton, wool, and linen. Also artificial cherry flavoring, artificial eggs, synthetic cheese. Nylon rope and plastic fence posts. None of these things can be made on farms, however, just real eggs, real sheep, real hemp for rope, etc., and with each prod of the finger another thousand farmers get squashed. I watch all this happening, and I am unable not to write about it.

The fourth kind of essay is altogether cheerier. Every once in a while I get to thinking about New England, and why it is the way it is, and pretty soon I find myself writing a meditation. There are two of them in this book.

Finally, of the roughly hundred book reviews I've written in the past decade, five are focused on rural life in ways that made me decide to include them in this book. I haven't segregated them in a section by themselves—what matters about them is not that they are book reviews, but that they formed lawful occasions to talk about ponds or woodlots or the best bedtime reading for gardeners. I have put each one where it ought to go.

There is one other thing to say before I let the book begin. I mentioned two farms. My new wife had a small place of her own when I met her; she has it still. One day we will both live full-time on one place or the other. Meanwhile, both are home. We keep a tractor at each place, and take turns mowing fields. There is a brisk flow of firewood, hay, wall-stones, etc., in both directions, depending on whether we're living more at North Farm (her place) at a given moment, or more at mine. This back-and-forthness accounts for a certain duality that may be apparent in some of the essays here.

NOEL PERRIN
*South Farm*
June, 1991

# Contents

ॐ

# Contents

## IV

### FINDING NEW ENGLAND

## V

### COUNTRY BATTLES

## VI

### THE (PARTLY) HAPPY ENDING

# ∾ I ∾
# Starting in Kansas

# 778 Prizes for Sheep

### ∾

LAST YEAR ABOUT 13 million people attended professional football games, and 23 million more went to symphony concerts. Nearly 130 million, however, went to state, regional, and county fairs. There was a day in North Carolina when the North Carolina State Fair was the fourth largest city in the state. There were numerous days when the ascending order of size of human agglomerations in Ohio went: Dayton, Akron, Ohio State Fair, Toledo.

The Kansas State Fair is not one of the giants. Even on a good day there may be no more than 50,000 people on the grounds. But it is one of the most thoroughly American — as befits the fair of our central state, the one that occupies the geographical heart of the country.

Consider. State fairs began basically as cattle and sheep shows. The fairgrounds in Hutchinson, Kansas, swarm with cows and sheep. Long ago they added entertainment. On one day at last year's Kansas fair I counted 172 different modes of entertainment, from car races to a 4-H fashion show to avant-garde theater. Right now foreign exhibits are in fashion at many state fairs. In Hutchinson I saw not only Governor Carlin of Kansas but also Governor He (you pronounce it Huh) Zhukang of Henan Province, China. Henan is the biggest wheat-producing region of China, as Kansas is of the United States, and that's how the two got together. Governor He was there with a delegation of thirty

3

Chinese officials to open the fair's first foreign trade exhibit. But despite the avant-garde theater troupe and the Chinese pavilion, this fair remains totally unpretentious. It has a down-home quality that sometimes gets lost at bigger fairs — and even sometimes at much smaller ones.

The Kansas fair runs for ten days in early September: nine regular days and one extra tacked onto the front. That's called Preview Day, and admission to the grounds is free so as to encourage people to pour in and get the fair off to a lively start. The other nine days you pay $2.50 to enter. I chose to arrive on Preview Day, because I like to see things begin. Within two hours I knew I was in luck. Coming from New England, where there are lots of small, local fairs and a mere handful of big ones, I had evolved three criteria for judging the down-homeness — you might even say the authenticity — of a fair.

One is food. All fairs sell large quantities of junk food. In fact, fairs probably invented junk food. The people who work at them were supplying an eager public with cotton candy and fried dough long before fast-food chains were dreamt of.

But the best fairs also have plenty of good home-made food. Quite often it's church food. You can tell when a fair has gone commercial by the decline in the number of booths selling home-made baked goods, by the disappearance of suppers put on by local groups.

Another is the proportion of volunteer workers. No fair worth its salt can be staffed entirely by volunteers, because a good fair needs a midway, and a midway that involves much more than throwing darts at balloons needs to be operated by professional carnival workers. Who else has access to Ferris wheels and Tilt-a-Whirls? But when the booths *and* the rides come to be operated by bored carnies, you know that the fair has ceased to command the loyalty of its community.

The third is the ratio of participants to spectators: the higher the ratio, the more genuine the fair. A tribal ceremony would be the ultimate in genuineness, since the entire tribe participates and no one is merely a spectator. That never happens at an American fair, but some come close. The month before coming to Kansas I'd been to the fair in Chelsea, Vermont — a special, fancy one celebrating the two-hundredth anniversary of the town. The immense parade down the main street of Chelsea had so many of the townspeople in it that there were only a couple of hundred left to watch. Even I, though not from Chelsea, was there as a participant; I was one of the float judges.

By all three criteria, the Kansas fair is authentic. When I reached Hutchinson, later on Preview Day than I'd meant to, I checked into a local motel and went right over to the fairgrounds to check things out — and to get something to eat. I wasn't about to waste my appetite on the Holiday Inn.

Strolling in through Gate 12, the first thing I passed was a cluster of gigantic horse trailers. The light constructions you see being pulled along behind station wagons in horse-show country would not give you a correct idea of these. These were trailers that could hold a small elephant. What they actually held were workhorses with hooves the size of dinner plates — two horses per trailer. One of the main events of the first regular fair day is the draft-horse pull, and the participants were beginning to arrive. Men and women in cowboy hats were unloading Belgians and Clydesdales, pulling out hay bales, checking harnesses. There were more very large horses than I had ever seen in one place before.

Next I passed the Sheep and Swine Barn, already filled. Then a building devoted entirely to rabbits. Soon — I have a sure instinct for food — I came to a cluster of eating places. Some were commercial, but the three that caught my eye were all church. In a small white building, an all-male contingent from Our Lady of Guadalupe was busy serving tacos and frijoles to a mixed crowd of Kansas farmer-types and teenage couples. Fifty yards away, side by side, were the larger eating places run by the Central Christian

School (of Hutchinson) and the United Methodist Church (of South Hutchinson).

I know Methodist food intimately. Vermont is well supplied with Methodists, and I have been to numerous suppers put on by them — have even worked in the kitchen at a few. One can nearly always count on a good meal. Even at times of peak demand —say, during fall-foliage season, when many supper organizers get over-whelmed by the sheer volume of tourists and take to serving pie with a crust made from mix, or actually going to a store and *buying* the dinner rolls — even then, Vermont Methodists go right on making the crust from scratch and kneading the bread dough. It was the work of an instant to decide to sample the Methodist cuisine of Kansas.

When I went inside, I found myself in a large white rectangular space. There were six tables, each holding sixteen people, and a serving line at the back. Five of the tables were full, and there were only a few places left at the sixth, even though it was now past dinnertime. I asked the people in front of me in line what I ought to get.

"Chicken with noodles and raisin cream pie, don't you think, Fred?" the wife answered. So I did. Delicious, both. Real crust on the pie, and real cream, too. It would pass muster in Union Village, Vermont.

Sitting there eating my chicken and noodles, I had plenty of time to look around — at the Bible quotations on the walls, the printed graces up and down the red-checked tablecloth, and the sign that said "God deserves our best." I also noticed another, more secular sign. This one noted that at the previous year's fair, the women of the church had baked 2,045 pies. Wow! That's roughly 2,000 pies more than I'm used to — that's down-home food on a truly gargantuan scale. (I never said the Kansas fair was small; it's only small compared with giants like the Texas State Fair, which on some days is larger than Trenton, New Jersey, and Wilmington, Delaware, combined.)

When I had finished the last crumb of my pie, I slid out past a

6

remarkably thin farmer who had three pieces, all different, laid out in front of his noodles. Then I ambled back to the Sheep and Swine Barn. The midway was going full tilt — a cacophony of music and recorded spiels. I was tempted to try a rollercoaster, or maybe even look in on one of the two freak shows and see the lobster people. But I raise a few sheep and pigs myself, and state fairs did begin with animals, a century and a half ago. I decided to start there.

By now it was nine P.M. Pigs like their sleep. What you'd have seen on the swine side of that huge barn were hundreds of recumbent pigs. They were sleeping two to a pen, and quite often one pig would have an affectionate trotter resting on the other pig. Occasionally a small group of people would walk through, quietly commenting on a handsome Duroc or Berkshire. It was sort of like night rounds at an old-fashioned hospital, where there are wards.

By contrast, the sheep side of the barn was all noise and activity. The exhibiting of farm animals has changed a lot since the first state fair, held in Syracuse, New York, in 1841. (There was an attempt to start a New Jersey state fair as early as the seventeenth century, and George Washington tried his hand at encouraging fairs in 1796. But the New York State Fair — it's still at Syracuse — is generally agreed to be the true beginning.)

Of course farmers groomed their animals back then — and there were plenty to groom. On one train alone, twenty-five carloads of livestock arrived in Syracuse in 1841. But what was then amateur beauty treatment has now become professional. All over the sheep side of the barn were slender metal stands, each with a fancy head-grip at the top. To each stand was tied a reluctant sheep, its head held high. Owners busily trimmed their coats with electric shears and gave them sponge baths. Hundreds of other sheep watched, most wearing canvas overcoats — not because it's cold in Kansas in September, but to keep them clean. Almost every sheep steadily baaed. In the distance you could hear five kinds of midway music. The pigs slept through it all.

From there I went next door to the Horse Arena, empty as yet

7

of draft horses. Instead there was one lone cowboy out in the arena and maybe fifty people in the stands watching him. In front of him a blonde young woman in a red shirt darted from side to side and as she darted, he wheeled his horse. I had to ask one of the spectators what was going on.

"He's practicing for the Open Championship Cutting," my neighbor said. When I still looked blank, he explained that there were five different competitions in which a rider's job was to separate one cow from a herd. "That's his wife," he went on; "she's playing the critter." As I later learned, there are a total of 308 horse competitions at the fair. A far cry from the first New York State Fair, which featured a single plowing contest.

Leaving the cowboy still wheeling, I followed the noise from this now mostly dark side of the fair over to the brilliant midway. I was still too full of dinner to be tempted by the homemade cake and candy being sold by teenage members of the Apostolic Faith Tabernacle. I did ride the Ferris wheel, from whose top I could see into the main grandstand, where close to eight thousand people were listening to a concert by the Beach Boys. I tried a couple of other rides. I proved too squeamish to go in and see the lobster people, though I listened entranced to the recorded spiel out front: "They're reeel! They're a-lahv! Ten thousand dollars reward if they're not reeel and not a-lahv! They have claws instead of hands. They have flippers instead of feet. Fahv generations of their kind have baffled medical science." I also talked to a young carnival worker from Texas, who advised me to be sure to have some Methodist food the next day. He said he himself began to think about chicken and noodles when he was still three fairs away.

As I see it, state fairs have passed through four stages in their history, and I'd already had glimpses of all four in Kansas. In the first stage, a very brief one, fairs were entirely for farmers and they were almost wholly educational. You went there to learn how to plow better, or to look at new farm machinery, or maybe to win

8

a small cash prize for your cattle or carrots. That hasn't changed. You still do these things, if you're a farmer or a 4-H kid. There were three carrot prizes awarded at the Kansas fair — nothing to make a person rich at $3 for best carrots, then $2 and $1, but still prizes. There were also 778 sheep prizes (mostly in the $4 to $18 range), 6 turnip prizes, 27 hay prizes, 92 apple prizes, and so on.

But there is a certain lack of drama to carrots or even (unless you're a farmer) to a display of new farm machinery. Fair organizers quickly discovered that it's hard to draw really big crowds unless you add a bit of frivolity to your educational enterprise. Since state fairs were cropping up all over the place in the mid-nineteenth century, there were lots of organizers around to make the discovery. So within a few years they added two new elements: politicians and fast horses. That marked the beginning of stage two.

The politicians, of course, came to make speeches, just like governors Carlin and He in Kansas. Daniel Webster and Henry Clay were both star attractions in the late 1840s. A bit later, President Grant canceled appearances two years running at my own state fair in Vermont, causing a local journalist to write somewhat bitterly, "It is a settled fact that public men do not always keep their promises." Journalists discover this once a generation.

The fast horses originally came to be put through their paces in exhibitions of fancy riding and "trials of speed." A top attraction at the Iowa fair in 1854 was the competition for "boldest and most graceful female equestrian." Prize: a gold watch. Educational value for farmers: zero. Interest: intense. The crowd got so excited that when judges gave the prize to what people considered the wrong young woman, there was a near riot. The spectators collected a purse of $165 (equivalent to maybe $5,000 now) for their candidate — and gave her a college scholarship as well.

It is hard to bet on exhibitions of fancy riding, however; soon the horses began to race for money. What ensued was probably

9

the most corrupt period in the history of state fairs. The education of farmers was never quite forgotten, and politicians kept coming to speak, but horse races dominated most fairs in the late nineteenth century. Many of the races were fixed, and sometimes the people who fixed them also ran the fair. In Minnesota in the 1880s the state fair was accused of becoming a private enterprise run for the benefit of the Twin City Jockey Club. When farmers complained and asked for more attention to sheep and carrots, the gamblers in Minneapolis and St. Paul could hardly contain their laughter. "Let 'em have a fair run on Sunday-school lines," said a Jockey Club official. "There won't be enough people there to trample down the grass."

He was wrong. The wrath of farmers and the concerted efforts of farm magazines did eventually restore the fairs to respectability, though it took a generation. (As late as 1902, the novelist William Dean Howells went to an Eastern fair, which he carefully did not name, and was aghast. "There was not one honest start in all the races at that fair," he wrote indignantly.)

And when the gambling died, the grass stayed well beaten down. What kept the crowds coming was a wonderful French invention called the Midway Plaisance. It first appeared in America in 1893. The original elements, all but one, were direct borrowings from abroad: the balloon rides, the belly dancers, the first primitive rollercoaster. To these the organizers of the World's Columbian Exposition in Chicago added one local attraction that has since become almost the symbol of American fairs. George Ferris of Illinois built the first Ferris wheel, and it was an instant success.

By the turn of the century most state fairs had a thriving midway, and had assumed the form later immortalized by the movie *State Fair*, starring Jeanne Crain and the state of Iowa. They have that form still, though there has been one major addition, which led to the present stage four. More about that soon.

I got up early, and over the next two days I indulged in a kind of

orgy of fairgoing. One morning was really early: I arrived at four
A.M. to catch the predawn action at the Milking Parlor. (Not much
of a crowd — to be precise, just me. Visitors nearly always prefer
the afternoon milking.) Some hours later I had an outstanding
pancake breakfast at a stand run by the First Congregational
Church of Hutchinson. Then I spent a long time in the giant
farm-exhibit building known as the Pride of Kansas, visiting with
the judges of hay and corn and with members of the all-female
support group for the Kansas cattle business known as the Cow-
Belles. (If you think that's demeaning, I hardly dare tell you
there's another group called the Porkettes. The members needn't
be the least bit overweight. They just like pigs.) I stuffed myself
with tacos at Our Lady of Guadalupe. I watched a performance of
Complex Improvisational Theater and another of the State Fair
Promenaders. I rode Dodg'em cars.

And I ate and ate. For lunch one day I bought a porkburger at a
volunteer stand and topped it off with a corn dog from one of the
dozen or so commercial corn dog stands. Then I had a jaffle,
which was not such a good idea. A Vermont waffle with maple
syrup is several orders of magnitude better. After eating most of
the jaffle, I waddled off to watch a set of stock-car races, regretting
that I wouldn't be there the day they were going to have a demoli-
tion derby featuring farm combines.

I also kept meeting more participants. I got to know a Kansas
sheep farmer named Chuck Woodard, who keeps almost exactly a
hundred times as many sheep as I do, and who was head chef at a
lamb barbecue the sheep exhibitors put on. Visitors from Vermont welcome. I went back to the Methodists one afternoon to
sample more kinds of pie and got to know Lyle Case, head of the
two hundred or so volunteers who run the cafeteria, sixteen or
eighteen to a shift, four shifts a day for ten days. I even had a
chance to meet a couple of the sixty prisoners from the Kansas
State Industrial Reformatory who volunteer to clean up the fairgrounds each morning. (We are a wasteful culture. They got ten

dumptruck loads from the grandstand alone, the morning after the Beach Boys concert.) These men earn $1.09 a day, and they fight for the privilege. For ten years no prisoner has attempted to escape while at the fair.

But two events stand out. One represents the still-vital rural past of state fairs, the other their urban, show-biz present. One full morning I spent in the packed stands of the Horse Arena, watching the draft horse pull. About fifteen hundred other people were also watching: teenaged girls in pink T-shirts as well as farmers in Stetsons and dark blue overalls. Nineteen teams were competing. What each had to do was pull a sort of sled loaded with fifty-pound salt blocks. To start things even, to handicap the event as one would say in the thoroughbred world, each team began by pulling exactly its own weight. One of the larger teams of Belgians would thus start out pulling 3,000 pounds of salt blocks; a small team might have only 2,600. Out in the arena there was a group of men to throw on extra salt blocks, or take them off, as each team backed up to the sled.

In this kind of pulling contest, you get three tries to move the sled ten feet forward. All nineteen teams pulled their own weight with ease; none needed the full three tries. For the next round the handlers added a thousand pounds to each team's weight, and for the third, another five hundred. Every team managed both of these rounds.

Meanwhile, the audience was getting a sense of the drivers: whether he (or in one case she) could *talk* the horses into lunging their hardest, or had to use a whip; whether after a pull he dashingly rode the whiffletree on around the arena like a Roman charioteer whose chariot had happened to disintegrate or just clutched the reins and ran alongside.

By 11:36 the load was up to own-weight plus 3,000 pounds, and there were only three teams left. At this moment a series of events occurred that sums up one whole aspect of state fairs. One of the remaining teams got so excited, trying and failing to pull 6,200 pounds of salt that when the horses were unhitched from the sled, they kept right on lunging. They very nearly crashed into the stands.

There was no panic, but there *was* a moment's confusion — and the busy salt handlers forgot to add 150 pounds for the next team. This was hard luck for Gene Boyd of Redfield, Kansas, not to mention Pat and Duke, his giant horses. When you get up to several tons, there's a rule of thumb that says if a team doesn't pull five or six feet on the first lunge, there's no way they'll make it up to ten on the next two, because that first heave takes so much out of the horses. Three blocks light, Pat and Duke got eight feet, six inches on their first lunge — a spectacular pull. But it's disqualified, and they must start over, with the correct weight and only two pulls left. On the first of these two, they make a scant three feet.

"Hard luck, Gene," the announcer calls — and for the first time the crowd mutters a little. The announcer, who's been calling the horse pull for twenty-five years, stops dead. He looks around. "All right," he says. "It's partly my fault. But Gene's a good sport, and I know he's going to accept my judgment."

Gene says nothing. Certainly he doesn't throw his racket down, or scream for a new umpire. He brings Pat and Duke around for the third and last pull. He clucks to them. They give a mighty heave — and pull the remaining seven feet. At one minute to twelve Gene has won the pulling contest and a purse of $210. Good guys sometimes finish first at the Kansas State Fair.

The other event that stands out was a concert. It differed in almost every way from the horse pull. That was daytime; this is at night — the warm Kansas night, full of locusts singing and young couples courting. That was a local thing and inexpensive; this is national and rather pricey. That was low tech; this is high.

On the fair's third night, I joined 3,700 other people in the main grandstand to listen to country music. George Strait and his Texans were the warm-up; Loretta Lynn and the Coalminers were the main show. For an afternoon performance plus this, Strait picked up $9,000. Loretta Lynn got $25,000, plus seventy percent

13

of the gate over $65,000. Because of the relatively slim crowd, her seventy percent didn't yield much — just another $10,000. It was still rather more than she would have gotten in the Horse Arena, or with Grand Prize carrots.

The grandstand faces due east. A huge moon was rising as we took our seats. It was tinged with red, said to be caused by prairie fires to the north. Big as that moon looked, though, it was not nearly as big as the loudspeaker in front of my section of stand. That was something out of science fiction. A stupendous rectangular boxlike thing, it hovered twenty feet up in the air, supported by a giant metal arm. It appeared to have six speakers in it. It easily produced more noise than a supersonic jet taking off.

Almost stunned with sound as I was, I didn't particularly enjoy the concert, though the accompanying light show had its moments. I did enjoy the eager response of the mostly young audience in the stands. They were prepared to love every song, to shout and scream and stamp and whistle. A few even moaned. It is that kind of audience and that kind of onlooker enthusiasm that has sustained state fairs over the last forty years.

Why? Because the thrill of the Midway Plaisance didn't last forever. By 1950 state fairs were in trouble again. Attendance was dropping (as was the farm population of the United States). The fairs continued to offer plenty of relaxed pigs, junk food, visiting politicians, horse and car racing, and Ferris wheels. But that wasn't enough. The increasingly nonrural customers wanted something more, only nobody knew what.

Then the general manager of the Ohio State Fair discovered what it was. Today the Ohio fair is the biggest of them all, but back then it almost foundered. The fall of 1952 was the low spot. The fair had lost money that year — the then-considerable sum of $58,000 — and there was talk of closing it. The general manager had a bold idea. What Daniel Webster and General Grant were in the nineteenth century, he reasoned, movie stars were in the twentieth.

When the fair opened in 1953, he had inaugurated stage four. A native of Ohio named Roy Rogers was on hand, fresh from Hollywood. Twice a day, every day, he did a show. The crowds picked up instantly, and the 1953 fair made money.

Naturally all the other managers were watching. Very soon the Wisconsin fair offered Rogers $234,000 to come up there and do a similar gig. He went, with the same happy result. Soon it struck fair managers that almost any big-time performer would do — it didn't have to be Roy Rogers and his horse. It also struck them that it would be better to have ten different celebrities during a ten-day fair, instead of recycling the same one day after day. The state fair as it now exists had come into being.

Obviously it won't stay frozen in its present form forever. Somewhere, stage five is waiting to happen. But what form will it take? Well, real courage is needed to predict. Predictions made at or about state fairs have a long history of being wrong. Horace Greeley was one of the attractions of the 1865 Minnesota fair; he gave a speech. In that speech he freely made predictions. One was that Minnesota farmers would soon be able to control rainfall by firing heavy artillery in the air. It hasn't happened yet. Another was that there would never be any decent apple pie in the state. "I should like to live in Minnesota but for one thing. You will never be able to raise apples here." Returning in 1871 for a second gig, he found his remark painted on a huge banner. Under it was an exhibit of one hundred varieties of Minnesota-grown apples.

But I'm not afraid. I'll prophesy. Stage five is going to be another redemption of state fairs. Not from failure, because they aren't failing, but from the growing inauthenticity that has crept over them (Kansas less than most) during the past forty years. Once farmers redeemed the fairs from their nineteenth-century decline into dishonest gambling venues. Now a different kind of farmer will pull them back from their gentler twentieth-century descent into triviality, spectatorhood, and pop-stardom.

State fairs began as learning holidays for farmers. That was what George Washington had in mind; that was what the New York State Fair provided in 1841. They were comparable to the kind of college reunion, increasingly popular in the 1990s, where the alums take seminars during the day and drink only in the evening.

It is to this learning-in-a-festive-atmosphere format that I think fairs will return — and it is the revolution in agriculture that will cause them to do it. The organic revolution I mean, of course. All over the United States, new people are moving into small-scale agriculture, and the vast majority of them intend to be either organic or very low-input farmers. They know they have a lot to learn. Fairs are a good place to learn some of it. Already the new agriculturists have organized fairs of their own — there is a particularly famous one in Maine. They are just now beginning to get the attention of that part of the agricultural establishment that controls state and county fairs. One of the great organic triumphs of the 1980s was to crack open the curriculum at state agricultural colleges, which for many years pretended there was no such thing as organic farming, and which now almost to a college offer courses in it. One of its triumphs in the nineties, I predict, will be to give a renewed sense of purpose and a heightened degree of participation to state fairs.

I can hardly wait to try my first organic porkburger when I go back to Kansas.

[1985]

# ❧ II ❧
# The Practical Farmer

# In Praise of Old Equipment

❧

A WHOLE INDUSTRY HAS GROWN up to serve part-time farmers. By "to serve" I mean primarily to sell us things. Suppose one of us owns a farm with an old hayfield behind the house. Suppose he or she wants to mow it some inexpensive way — maybe by hand. Real farmers haven't hand-mowed for three generations, and the necessary tools almost vanished. Because of us they have returned, nicely updated. At least two companies are waiting to supply all the equipment we'll need: a good Austrian scythe blade, a good American snathe, a wooden hay rake with nylon teeth, a hay cart. . . .

On the other hand, suppose one of us has a little more money and a little less time, and wants to go after a hayfield with modern equipment. At least five companies are lined up to lure us with a small but genuine tractor, a proper-looking machine with big rear wheels, a power takeoff, and the ability to handle a six-foot cutter bar. Dozens of other companies build dozens of other things intended just for us: prefab barns for the two-cow farm, pint-size wagons, even miniature bulldozers.

It is no wonder there is such an industry, because we are quite a market. There are just over a million American farmers, me included, whose principal occupation is something other than farming. Four-fifths of us work at our nonfarm jobs two hundred or more days a year. We annually bring somewhere around $25 billion back from town with us. No one knows how much of it we spend buying new farm equipment, as opposed to pouring it into real estate taxes or doing ordinary nonfarm things like going out to dinner. But clearly it's a lot. I seldom meet a part-time farmer who goes a whole year without buying some new piece of equipment. I meet many who seem to get something new and shiny about every three months.

It used to be that I did that myself — nor is the temptation gone yet. I freely admit that I still feel passionate yearnings when I see a persuasive ad for some new kind of mini-harrow, a cute thing designed for an operation just my size. Sometimes I do more than yearn. Sometimes I rush out and buy one, as I did with the harrow.

But quite often I resist. Of course I still buy just as many things — no farmer ever has enough tools. But at least half of what I now buy is real farm equipment, one to two generations old, not new mini-machines. It's a change in pattern I've come to through bitter experience.

The bitterest happened five years ago. I needed a manure spreader. I had recently enlarged my herd of beef cattle . . . from three head to five. Even when there were only three, they had produced quite a respectable pile of manure each winter. Enough to keep me busy for several days in the spring. I had other stuff to spread, too. We heat with wood, and we have an oversized, under-insulated house. (It's an old brick one, and hard to retrofit.) The woodburning furnace and the stoves produce quite a respectable quantity of ashes. Provided you're careful not to use too many of those brightly colored advertising inserts that come in most news-papers as part of your kindling, wood ashes do all sorts of good to hayfields. But it is tedious to scatter them from a bucket.

Back in three-cow days I had a simple arrangement. Come spring, I would ask my neighbor Floyd Dexter for the use of his spreader, a big old ground-driven one. Then I'd spend a hectic couple of days loading (by hand, with a manure fork), spreading, loading again. I'd add a few bucketfuls of ashes to each load.

But manure-spreading does the most good, as every farmer knows, if you do it just before — or during — a gentle rain, so that all that ammonia soaks into the ground. It usually worked out that the couple of days I had Floyd's spreader were hot and sunny, and off went my ammonia on the breeze. Not satisfactory. Then one year, hurrying to get a last load out before dark, I managed to break one of the beaters on his machine. He was without his spreader for nearly a month, while the dealer I took it to waited for parts.

That did it. I decided the time had come to buy my own. A new one the size of his would cost $4,000. Absurd for something I'd use two days a year — maybe three, now that I had so many cows. Fortunately, I'd been seeing ads all over the place for a cute little mini-spreader you could order by mail. That cost only $600. Off went my check.

A week later the box of parts came. (Somehow I had imagined the whole thing ready to use, the way it looked in the ads.) But except that the wheels were about the size of large doughnuts, a detail that had escaped me in the ads, they seemed like perfectly satisfactory spreader parts. With a little help from Floyd, I got the thing assembled the next day, and I hitched it to my big old tractor. It *was* mini, all right. The combination looked ridiculous, as if a real locomotive were pulling one of the toy railroad cars they have at some amusement parks. Floyd couldn't resist a grin. Oh, well. I hadn't bought the spreader to make some kind of macho statement; I just wanted to get my fields fertilized. The next rainy day I would do it.

Tuesday of the following week was perfect: a day of light drizzle. Soon after dawn I had my tractor and spreader drawn up next to the hay feeder where my cattle had been dropping their manure all winter. I was dying to play with my new machine. I figured I'd have time for at least three loads before I had to leave for work.

It took maybe fifteen minutes to load the little thing, and off I went in the rain to start spreading. The tractor rolled along, the spreader followed — and nothing at all happened. Not one lump of manure came flying out. About the third time I stopped, checking anxiously to see what mistake Floyd and I had made in assembly, I realized that we hadn't made any. The apron simply wasn't moving. A full load of manure was beyond the machine's strength. It had jammed.

So I walked back to the hay feeder, got the manure fork, and proceeded to spread about half my load by hand. I climbed on the tractor and moved forward for another test. Still nothing happened. I hand-spread half of what was left, got back on the tractor, and moved ahead in second gear. Now finally the manure began to fly. The beaters were small, and they certainly didn't produce that sort of manure cloud that Floyd's old spreader did — but never mind. I was getting the pasture fertilized on a rainy morning, and if I had to do it in many small loads, that was all right, too. Next load I'd add a few ashes.

At that moment there was the sound of metal breaking. I had been spreading for perhaps forty feet. I stopped the tractor for the fifth time, climbed down, and went back to find that a little cog arm had snapped under the weight of even a quarter load. (The manufacturer did replace it free — even sent me two.) I pitched out the rest of the load with the manure fork, and drove back to the barn in disgust. Eventually I borrowed Floyd's spreader again — and got my manure out mostly on one brilliantly sunny weekend, losing nearly all the ammonia.

I have since learned my machine's limits. It's fine for wood ashes, provided you don't fill it more than half full. Ashes are light and feathery. It might handle the fresh droppings of one horse. But a winter's worth of cow manure, well trodden and mixed with hay, it simply does not have the strength to cope with. It is not a farm machine, and I should not have bought it. For half of the $600 it cost me, I could have bought a used farm spreader that really worked. It would have been old and rusty, but it would have had six different settings, so you could select how heavy a dressing you wanted to put down. It could have been filled to overflowing, load after load. It also undoubtedly would have broken sometime within the first year; probably some of the rusty apron links would have snapped. For the other half of what I paid, I could have had it nicely fixed — good for years to come.

That of course brings up one of the reasons people like me start out not even considering old equipment. We figure it will break down, and then what? Who's going to do this nice fixing? Certainly not us. Not me, anyway. I was born mechanically inept and raised in the kind of suburb where you call a plumber if you have so much as a dripping faucet. True, I've gained astonishingly in the twenty-five years I've had a farm, but I am not up to rural standard and never will be. I will never resemble my neighbor up the hill, Ed Paige, who can take one glance at a mowing machine that isn't mowing quite right and say casually, "Whyn't you try attaching the stabilizer arm?" I could study the thing for twenty minutes without even noticing there *was* a stabilizer arm. That sort of blindness makes a person cautious.

All the same, I now boldly buy rusty stuff. How come? Because I've tapped into the rural grapevine. In the old days, when something broke, I thought I had two choices. I could shamefacedly ask a neighbor for help, knowing that he wouldn't take pay, and knowing that I had no comparable skill to offer in return. Or I could go to the huge trouble and expense of getting the machine to a dealer who was probably twenty miles away. Sometimes something would go unfixed all summer because I hated to ask a friend to come over and tell me what was wrong and then put it right, when about all I could do in return would be to give him a cup of coffee and a doughnut.

Actually, there has been a third choice all along. The country has always been full of secret repair people. Professionals. True experts. They don't mean to be secret (usually); they just don't list themselves in the yellow pages, still less put out good money for ads in newspapers. It wouldn't be worth it, since they only do the repair work part-time, after a day's farming or construction work. One ad might eat up a week's profit.

Mostly they don't even put signs out in front of their houses — and that, I think, is because it doesn't occur to them. They're like the farmer an impatient friend of mine, a tough dowager, once tried to pass on a back road in West Fairlee, Vermont. She had made about five attempts, and was just swinging out for a sixth when, without signaling, he turned left into a driveway. She drove right in after him, furious at so nearly having had an accident.

"*Don't* you know enough to signal when you turn!" she cried, leaping out of her car, eyes blazing.

He climbed out of his pickup, just as mad. "Everyone around here knows where I live," he snapped, and without giving her a chance to make a second attack, stalked off into the barn.

Everyone on the grapevine knows where the secret repair people live — or at least they can find out. I joined the grapevine, in fact I almost became a grape myself, when I got appointed to our town's zoning board. There are seven of us on the board, and not much goes on in town that at least one of us doesn't hear about. Being connected is what we get, I suppose, instead of pay.

Thus when I finally decided to get a bucket-loader, a couple of years ago, I didn't even consider checking to see if there was a cute little model designed for people like me. Instead I checked the grapevine. Through it I heard about an old Ferguson tractor three towns away, which its owner would sell for $2,500. It had a hydraulic bucket mounted, state of the art for 1956 and still working well. It also had thirty-year-old tires, a worn clutch, and no instruction manual. I bought it.

Of course one of those old tires has already given out, and of course a giant tractor tire is beyond my competence to replace. But it's not past the competence of Sylva LaCasse, the genius welder who lives in the next village. Of course the engine has needed some work. Go a mile past Syl's place, and you come to

Ernest Clay's farm. Mr. Clay (if you ask him in the slack season for farming) will usually agree to fix an old tractor, and I expect he could do it blindfolded if he had to. Of course one of the ancient hydraulic hoses blew once, and of course I turned to Dave Fitzgerald, right up the road. Meanwhile, that old loader has moved rocks the size of chest freezers, picked up pine sawlogs as if they were pencils, taken over the manure loading, easily hoisted a beef or two for butchering. It is in better shape now than when I got it. It even *looks* better. My skill does extend to painting.

I don't claim that old-is-good applies in every case. I wouldn't dream, for example, of getting some clunky old chainsaw from the sixties. Shiny new ones are preferable in every way. I do claim that for many kinds of farm equipment it makes sense to buy something heavy-duty, with fifty or a hundred years of prior models behind it, not something new and light and untried.

We innocent farmers need experienced equipment.

[1986]

# A Pond of One's Own

ᕉ

PLAYING WITH WATER IS one of the pleasures all children understand. Put a child near a mud puddle. If there's a way to drain it by
digging a little canal, he will. Take the child to the beach. He'll be
digging sand-pools in no time. Give him access to a small brook.
He's nearly certain to dam it.

This pleasure carries very readily over to adult life. Not often in
pure form, to be sure. Most grown-ups would feel foolish if they
sat down on the beach and started excavating a string of ponds
with a toy shovel. They'd look even sillier draining mud puddles
with a stick. But the impulses to impound water and to set it
flowing remain, and in the right circumstances they will — so to
speak — come flooding out.

One of the most embarrassing moments of my own adulthood
occurred, for example, when I thought I was alone in an abandoned rice paddy. I was twenty-four years old and a first lieuten-
ant in the United States Army. A seasoned combat veteran, I'd
been fighting in Korea for nearly a year. Most of that time I had
been the reconnaissance officer of the 196th Field Artillery. I and
my seven men did the exploring and survey work whenever the
battalion moved.

Once when we were advancing and the North Koreans retreat-
ing, my men and I were out looking for places to site a new assault
gun. I had them triangulate their way up from the old position,
and I went ahead by myself to check out three little valleys we had

just recaptured. One of them might do for the gun Sergeant Weis and the other six were to meet me in the central valley at noon, bringing the survey data and also the C-rations for our lunch.

They were late. There I stood: hot, hungry, and bored. All around me were terraced rice paddies, descending in two-foot steps down the valley. Except at the lower end, where there'd been a skirmish, they were full of water — eight or nine silent ponds.

Two feet is a nice drop. It seemed a pity not to have a little waterfall, or, better yet, a series of them. I had no shovel — no tools at all but a loaded carbine, and the regulation pistol strapped on my belt. I certainly wasn't going to dig up rice paddies with either of *them*. But fingers came before forks, and hands before handguns. As all small children know, the cupped hand does just fine in soft mud, provided you don't mind a little dirt under your fingernails. Completely forgetting my dignity, I squatted down and began excavating a spillway from the top paddy into the next lower one.

When I became conscious some time later that I was being watched, I looked up — and there stood my little detachment, all seven of them, clean and soldierly. Me, I was on my hands and knees, pretty well covered with mud, and the second waterfall just nicely started. "You shoulda been a farmer, sir," Sergeant Weis said with a perfectly straight face.

Weis was even righter than he knew. Of all grown-ups, farmers get to play with water most — and no one laughs at them, either. Like firemen (who get to play with water second-most), and like physicists and poets, farmers do real work that happens also to have a sportive element.

Farmers make waterbars to keep dirt roads from washing out. They dig irrigation canals and drainage ditches, often using heavy equipment. Best of all, they get to have farm ponds. A farm pond, of which there are said to be 2.2 million in the United States, is a wonderfully versatile thing. It's got more uses than a Swiss Army knife. It's fire protection. It's a home for fish. It's the family swimming hole. It's a source of stock water. In the north it can double as a hockey rink. Make the pond shallow enough, and you can even grow wild rice.

My own farm pond is not one of the more impressive ones. It probably doesn't even get counted among the 2.2 million. I hand dug it years ago at the front of the cow pasture, where there was a little boggy swale between two high banks. I consulted no one; I just went out and dug. The only swimming in the pond is done by frogs, and not many of them since the rain turned acid. But the cattle love it, and I love it, and my daughters pretty well lived in it when they were little. We never worried about their drowning. The deepest spot is about thirty inches, and the total length of the pond about twenty feet.

For larger ponds, you probably need machinery, and you certainly need technical advice. One source of that is Farmers' Bulletin 2256, "Building a Pond," published by the U.S. Department of Agriculture: useful, but brief and a shade bureaucratic. Another is a small book called *Earth Ponds*, which is one of the least bureaucratic books I have ever seen. In fact, it's written in a language which its enemies would call Mellowspeak, and which I myself would call Practical Zen. Or maybe Sensible Counterculture. It is full of good advice for pond-builders, especially those who don't want to spend a lot of money.

Tim Matson, the author, was part of that wave of young college graduates who moved to the country in the late sixties and early seventies. He and a woman friend bought a small farm in central Vermont. It had an old pond which they fixed up, and in which they began to raise rainbow trout. Then, as affairs do, theirs ended. "We sold the farm, split up the trout, and rambled off to chase our different fates."

His fate was another farm, just a few miles away. This one had neither brook nor pond, and hence no spiritual focus. Matson set out to remedy that at the lowest possible cost. He wound up spending $900. Today, he says, "I live in a homemade cabin overlooking a quarter-acre apple-green pond that I sited, cleared and carved in collaboration with a bulldozer sculptor. Happily, not long ago I hooked a mountain mermaid. Together we cultivate most of our own food and collect all our firewood and lumber, with some surplus left over to barter with neighbors in the hills. Seventy-five trout fatten in the pond, and surplus water gravity-feeds a rich market garden and a winter pig. Long-range pond schemes include a fire-fighters' pump, a small hydro generator, a wood-fired sauna, and an ice house. Our holding will swell with pond power."

If that description makes you sigh with envy, then you may want to read the book and learn how to enjoy pond power yourself. Along with quite a lot of oriental poetry (about ponds) and half a dozen apt quotations from that pioneering European work, *A New Book of Good Husbandry . . . Conteining the Order and Manner of Making Fish-Pondes* (London: 1599), Matson has full and practical advice on how to pick a pond site, how to decide what size the pond should be, how to keep it from leaking, when you need a permit, how to make a brook excavate a "digger pond" for you at no cost whatsoever, and so on. The one thing he doesn't tell is how to hook mountain mermaids. But some things people have to learn for themselves.

Reading Matson's book has already caused me to make one change in my own miniature pond. Like most Americans, I instinctively seek total control of things. A constructed pond, something in my subconscious says, should be sort of like an outdoor bathtub. You fill it to the desired level, keep it there as long as you choose, add any bathsalts or bubble beads you wish. Whenever you want to, you let out all the water and wash the rim.

With these thoughts unconsciously present, I designed my pond so that it could be drained at any time. That is, I put a four-inch cast-iron pipe through the base of the dam, and corked the inside end with a four-inch wooden plug. If I ever wanted the pond empty, all I had to do was knock out the plug.

There's nothing foolish about wanting to empty a small pond. Even in the Middle Ages, monastic fish ponds were drained every few years for cleaning. In fact, they were often kept empty for two or three years, and crops grown in the fertile bed. Millet is said to do best. You can control pond weeds that way; and if undesirable fish have moved in, you get rid of them.

The foolish part, I now see, was in automatically opting for a built-in drain. In a loose-earth dam, at least, it just causes trouble. As Matson points out several times (the book is a little repetitious), you are almost certainly going to have seepage around the drain-pipe, even if you or your builder puts a collar on it. Earth and metal just don't form a tight seal. Even in my tiny pond, with very low water pressure, there tended to be seepage. On the occasions when some clumsy cow managed to stumble over the protruding end of the pipe and stir it in its bed, there wasn't just seepage, there were horrible big leaks.

According to Matson, the thing to do is to forget about plumbing fixtures when you build a pond; leave that for houses and maybe for the engineers at Hoover Dam. Instead, buy a roll of flexible plastic pipe, and keep it in the barn. Then if the time comes when you want to drain your pond, you deftly siphon the water over the top of the dam.

According to some skeptics I know, Matson has failed to take into account the fact that much of the United States is quite level. One pond-builder told me with eyes flashing that if he'd used a siphon it would have had to be half a mile long. But at least for hillside ponds, the idea makes sense to me.

Matson has lots of other ideas, nearly all of which I find appealing. Some year soon I may have my own quarter-acre pond, with eight feet of water at the deep end, and a school of trout to eat the bugs. I'm only sorry I don't know where Sergeant Weis and Sergeant Bevans and Sergeant Boehnan are, so I could invite them to come over and play waterfall with me.

[1984]

# Hands Across the Pasture

❧

TWO LITTLE GIRLS, their arms a whir of motion, are slowly walking across my front meadow. Fourteen cows watch them with mild curiosity. The cows are clustered on a knoll, resting. The little girls, bareheaded in the bright June sun, are working as hard as they can. Each girl is picking milkweed at top speed — pulling up stems with both hands simultaneously, dropping one plant and reaching for another in the same motion. This is a race. They are racing to see which one can pull up a thousand plants fastest.

I arranged that contest, one of many milkweed pick-offs that took place on my farm during the 1970s. My daughters Elisabeth and Amy were the original competitors. Later, after they became blasé adolescents, my stepdaughters Manon and Kiki took over. There was even a brief period in the middle when all four girls competed simultaneously. A lot of milkweed died. It was one part of a somewhat peculiar program of pasture control.

I won't, as a matter of conviction (or maybe just superstition) use herbicides. Neither will I plow my pastures. They're hilly, and I won't risk the erosion. One of them is so full of rocks that I can neither plow nor mow it anyway.

But you have to do *something* if you want to keep land open. You have to do quite a lot if, as I did, you get your place from a summer person who hasn't farmed it. When I bought this ninety-acre farm, every pasture but one was full of weeds and brush. Behind the house there was still a good seven-acre hayfield. But across the road, the twenty acres of fenced land were in a state of rapid devolution. Burdocks crowded the shady fencelines; goldenrod grew thickly everywhere. There were patches in the two best fields that seemed almost pure milkweed. I also had Indian pipestem, alias jointgrass, scattered thistles, a little of that angular vine called bedstraw. And the trees! Thousands of little poplar trees and wild cherries had moved into every pasture but the front one by the road. The young Scotch pine were not far behind. (They were escapees from a plantation half a mile away.) Of bushes the worst was a particularly thorny one, with bright yellow wood and roots, that I now know to be barberry. Considerable ground juniper, too. And, of course, lots of briars.

Merely repairing the fences and reintroducing cows eliminated many of the invaders. The cows were delighted to eat the leaves off the little popples and cherry trees, and about three years of losing all its leaves depresses even the most determined sapling. With less enthusiasm, the cows also ate the burdocks. They have delicately flicked the leaves off most of the wild blackberries that grow on the pasture hillsides; blackberries, though far from eliminated, are well under control. They ate the Indian pipestem and the bedstraw.

Plants that a cow won't eat but that are easy to kill by cutting, I cut. I mowed the pines and the ground juniper with a tractor where they were small enough and the ground level enough. I used clippers and chainsaw on the several thousand that were too big or that grew on slopes too steep for a tractor. At least you only have to do it once per Scotch pine, provided you cut low enough to get the very bottom branch, hiding in the grass. Unlike our native white pine, a Scotch can stay alive with a single branch — and in about five years turn that branch into an entire new tree, six feet high and growing fast.

As to the goldenrod, it simply vanished. Repeated mowing ought to be the explanation, but as it has also vanished on some slopes I've never had the courage to mow, I am inclined to share credit with the Herefords. I admit I have never once seen one of them eating goldenrod; maybe they only like its night flavor.

But that still leaves a number of plants that are extremely hard to kill and that no cow will touch. I'm thinking especially of milkweed and thistles and barberry bushes. I wound up evolving a different technique for each of the three.

Milkweed was the simplest. It's not thorny, and because it releases easily from its underground runners, even a small child can easily pick it. When I first got the farm, I didn't have a tractor and I did have small children.

Contests were no part of the original plan. I just had a standing offer for any child, resident or visiting. I would pay one cent for every five milkweed stems. Usually what happened was that a child would want to go to the store for a bite of junk food. (This farm is just a half-mile from the village, and child trips were frequent.) If a single child went out, he or she was likely to pick two or three hundred, and then get bored and stop, or maybe go to five hundred, so as to have earned a dollar. This usually took half an hour for a ten-year-old, somewhat longer for a younger child.

The race evolved by accident, when Elisabeth and Amy happened to be picking together, and began comparing totals; and I happened to be fixing fence within earshot. I offered a prize of twenty-five cents to whichever one reached a thousand first. The whir of arms instantly began, the picking rate doubled, and even the loser was not too disappointed, since she found herself with two crisp new dollar bills for just over half an hour's work. Such races continued for almost a decade.

Milkweed of course comes right back, since picking it disturbs the roots not at all. But, then, desire to visit the store comes right back, too. Keep repicking, and you can wear the plants out. The first pasture got pretty well cleared in the first two years; and by the time Manon and Kiki became blasé teenagers, they were working steep slopes in the pasture farthest back, and grumbling that it took forty-five minutes or more to reach a thousand. Milk-weed still pops up here and there, and once or twice a summer I do a maintenance pick myself, for free. But its dominance is over. By actual count this past summer, there were sixty-three to pull in the first pasture, where once a little girl could get a thousand every day for a week and still have some left for future income.

Thistles, praise God, were always less numerous — a lucky break, since they are so much harder to deal with. In my early innocence I used to try cutting them, which I think just amuses thistles. Then, wearing heavy gloves, I began trying to pull them. In time I learned to wait until after a heavy rain, when the roots have trouble holding on to the moisture-lubricated earth. That does in fact work for thistles big enough to get a grip on but still so small as to be only semi-established. It has no effect at all on a large healthy thistle. Depressing. So depressing that one year I modified my no-herbicide policy a little. I tried two folk remedies. I cut forty large thistles at ground level, painted twenty of the stumps with kerosene, and loaded the other twenty with salt left over from curing sheepskins. One salted thistle died, along with many small rings of grass. I couldn't see that most of the rest were even slowed down in their regrowth. The next time I was in a hardware store I went so far as to read the label on a can of Roundup.

Then a neighbor showed me how to dethistle a pasture with a shovel. You dig the shovel in a couple of inches right next to the taproot, grab the stalk with one gloved hand, and with the other use the shovel as a lever. About three times out of four (when the ground is moist) you can get the whole root. Thistle maintenance and milkweed maintenance now take the same modest amount of time.

Barberry bushes I also used to try cutting. Indeed, there's no other way to get at the center of a big old one that has grown itself into a fortified circle five feet across — one solid mass of prickly stems.

But hacking one's way into Fort Barberry is not exactly like taking the Alamo. I mean, surrender is strictly temporary. Suppose that the year after General Santa Anna's victory, he had gone back to San Antonio for a visit and found that the Texans had mysteriously regarrisoned the place with more soldiers than before. Suppose that instead of Davy Crockett and 180 men, he found Davy Crockett's son and a fresh regiment of 1,000, grinning at him from the walls.

Barberry bushes are like that. Cut one of the thorny, yellow-wooded stems, and next year a little clump comes up in its place. Cut a whole bush, and next year you get a miniature forest. If barberry bushes grow in Greece, I expect they were the original inspiration for that myth about the hydra — the many-headed sea serpent which was just about invulnerable, because whenever you cut off one of its heads, it grew two new ones.

Hercules eventually got rid of the hydra by applying fire to each neck as soon as he whacked the head off, and a similar technique might work with barberry bushes. Decapitate the bush, make a brushpile on the site, and then (getting permission from the town fire warden) light a bonfire. It *might* work — and then again, as soon as the fire was out, several hundred yellow-wooded thorny sprouts might start on their way up from deep in the ground, where the heat never reached. It might also work to go around with a gallon of Roundup . . . if you don't mind dropping a little poison into the ecosystem.

What I know works for sure is to take a logging chain and wrap it around a barberry bush just below ground level. Then pull with truck or tractor until the whole serpentine mass of yellow roots gets torn out. Time required: maybe twenty minutes per large bush. (You have to dig a little while you're setting the chain.) Cost: nothing.

Does all this sound like the work of an obsessed perfectionist? Like someone who has confused twenty-seven acres of pasture with a suburban lawn or a putting green? Someone who has an irrational fear of chemical progress? It may be so. And yet consider what a sense of achievement, not to mention what a nice summer income those little girls got. Consider how well I know my land from thistle-hunting. I've seen fox cubs and whole families of raccoons and any number of deer when I was out at dawn, stalking thistles in the dew. And finally consider the profit to me. When I sell a side of beef, I can and do sell it as organic. There may be chemists, there may be feedlot owners and Burger King officials, who don't think organic beef is anything special. The public knows better. I can get about a twenty percent premium for what I sell. And as for the steaks I keep — not even those places that advertise direct shipment from Omaha have anything to match the flavor of a grass-fed organic steer.

[1986]

# A Truck with Pull

⁓

IT WASN'T A BIG firewood truck, but it wasn't tiny, either. Maybe you've seen one like it: a three-quarter or one-ton pickup that's been converted to a flatbed, so that it can deliver two cords at a time.

This one had both its right wheels in the ditch, a muddy ditch on the side of a back dirt road in a back Vermont town. Probably the driver had moved over six inches too far, trying to let someone past the other way.

"Need some help?" I called.

The driver, a heavy, bearded man in his thirties, eyed my little blue Toyota pickup. Perhaps he also noticed my white hair. "Yeah, thanks," he said. "Probably what I better do is go get my skidder."

"If you like. But I think I can pull you out."

Then I pointed to what he *hadn't* noticed: the electric winch mounted on the front of my little truck. He almost smiled.

"Maybe you could," he said. "Be nice. It'd save me 'bout eight miles."

So I drove on past him, turned around, and came back, staying as far on the other side of the road as I dared. I stopped about thirty feet short of him, carefully aiming the nose of my truck at the nose of his. Then I got out the four chocks I keep behind the seat. By now he was in the spirit of the thing — he took them and chocked all four of my wheels. Meanwhile, I rooted around for the winch control, which also lives behind the seat (along with a

37

six-foot logging chain, a pair of work gloves, and, effete touch, a large black umbrella.)

Leaving my engine running and the hand break set, I began to winch. It wasn't even hard. The winch groaned some, but it pulled him and his wood right back onto the road. Total time, including conversation: about seven minutes. After his ritual offer to pay and my equally ritual refusal, we went our ways.

My present truck is the fifth one I've owned, the second that was four-wheel drive, and the first with a winch. I can't imagine why I waited so long. I haven't had so much fun since I was a small boy playing with a toy steamshovel.

My new plaything is expensive. That I freely admit. When I bought the Toyota in the summer of 1987, I paid $13,000. More than $2,000 of that was for the winch.

Has it paid for itself? Of course not. I don't charge for my road services, and there haven't been many of them, anyway. Just that firewood truck, and once my sister-in-law's Bronco during an ice storm, and my daughter's car on the same hill during that same storm, and a friend's tractor in a boggy hayfield three years ago, and my own tractor last summer (I could hardly charge myself), and maybe two more. No profit there.

Only once has the winch produced a cash benefit of any size. That was when I had to take down a big dead maple last year. There's a row of old maples along the road in front of my house; back when they were planted it was a good place for a maple to be. But now they suffer from their proximity to road salt. They've been slowly weakening for twenty years, despite fertilizer, love, and — for a decade now — immunity from tapping. Last year one of the two biggest finally died.

It was not an easy tree to take down. If it fell back into the yard, the top would smash into my house. If it fell across the road, it would take the power lines and the phone lines. I've already knocked a power line down with a tree once in my life, and it's not an experience I'm anxious to repeat.

On the other hand, if this wide-crowned old tree fell to either side, it was sure to lodge in one of its neighbor maples, and a fine mess *that* would be. The only way that maple could safely fall was at an angle of about forty degrees in from the road, which would put the top near but not actually on my barn.

But how to accomplish that? Dead trees are much harder to take down than live ones, because instead of gradually bending on a hinge of green wood, they tend to snap at some unguessable point when you've almost cut through. Then they fall any way they please.

If I hadn't had an electric winch — and one with a hundred feet of cable, at that — I would have paid a tree company to come cut it. They, mindful of the house and the wire, would probably have cut it in sections, from the top down. It would have cost me $300, $400, maybe even $500. Instead, I just got a ladder and put a chain around the tree about twenty-five feet up. I parked the truck a hundred feet away at the forty-degree angle, and hooked on the cable. Then a neighbor ran the winch while I sawed. The tree landed within a foot of where I intended it to. Garrett, the neighbor, had brought his own chainsaw; he stayed and helped me buck the tree up. Total cost of removal: $0.00. Fair credit for winch: $400.

That still leaves $1,600 to amortize — and as I've already admitted, I can't. Not in cash. Try me on pleasure, though, and I might get as high as the equivalent joy of two weeks in a good hotel in Paris. Here are some of the things that keep me busy and happy with my winch.

My farm — my sort-of-farm, I should say — has one old pasture with a lot of well-rooted brush in it. Big mean stuff, often with thorns. The barberry bushes are, of course, the worst. Even yanking them out with truck and chain did not always work. I'd get the chain wrapped, hop in the cab, put the truck in first gear, and slam forward. One time in three or four, the bush would pull out, roots intact. Then the truck and I would shake hands, so to speak. More usually, the chain would slide up over the bush, and come loose in a shower of leaves. Or else the main root would snap. With the oldest and toughest bushes, nothing would happen at all except a nasty shock to the truck frame when the chain drew tight.

The winch has changed all that. With a winch one has exquisite control. I can tighten the chain so slowly that it seldom gets a chance to slip. If I do see it start to, I'm right there, I'm not in the cab of the truck. I can reposition it in about two seconds. With the hundred-foot cable I can pull barberries and firethorns off slopes where I'd never dare take the truck itself. Slope-picking requires a crew of two, of course: one down at the truck to run the control and one up at the bush setting chain. My wife loves winching as much as I do (she once said that if it weren't such a sexist phrase, she'd be glad to be called the winch wench), and on slope days she comes along with me. I don't mean to sound as if there were one of these every week. There have been maybe four in all.

Another thing the winch is good at is snaking logs out of inaccessible places. My farm is a hilly one, and the wooded parts are the hilliest of all. Some of its woody slopes are below field level, rather than above. It's quite handy to drive to the top of a bank that I have never gone down except on foot, hook on to a nice straight pine log forty feet below, and soon have that log on the pile, ready for the traveling sawmill that comes by every year or two.

But my favorite winching sport is moving entire trees. Making Birnam Wood come to Dunsinane, you might say.

The same rundown pasture that has all the thorn bushes also has a lot of bull pines in it. (Bull pine: a pine tree that grew up in an open field, and that therefore has huge branches right down to the ground. Sometimes called a wolf tree.) Years ago I took most of the little easy ones out. The few big ones that had a good log in them have been sawed up and turned to lumber. What that leaves are the twisted, knotted, weevil-bent big ones. Once or twice a year I get ambitious and decide to spend a day playing matador to a few bull pines.

Pine cuts almost like butter, if you have a well-sharpened chainsaw. Felling one of those trees takes only a few minutes. And even though it may have as many as fifty big limbs, cutting it up isn't going to take much over an hour. Well, a little more in my case, because I like to get something tangible out of the job (besides another three hundred square feet of pasture where grass will now grow). So any straight branch between about two and four inches in diameter gets converted into pieces of sugar wood: fuel for the little evaporator we use to make maple syrup. Still, even with that extra cutting and loading, two hours at the most.

But here's the problem. What I'm left with in the pasture is something like a whale after the *Pequod* has got through with it. The trunk and ninety-five percent of the branches of this enormous pine tree lie flopped across my pasture. If I waited ten or fifteen years, the branches would melt in by themselves, and the trunk would surely go in a century.

But I'm the impatient type; I want that stuff out *now*. I have two choices. I can make a huge brushpile, let it dry for a year, and burn it. The trunk won't burn, just char, but I can move that later, section by section, with the tractor. Or, right now, I can load all those branches onto my pickup, and drive a couple of hundred feet over to the fenceline. Then I can pitch them all over the stone wall into the edge of the woods. I used to do that. The branches of a big bull pine make something like eight truckloads.

But not any more I don't. Now I just reel out my winch cable and drag the whole tree over to the fence. Then I cut it up there, stopping at intervals to pitch branches over. Macho experiences are not something I usually seek. Macho experiences remind me too much of war. But I have to admit that it gives me a delicious power feeling to see a very large pine tree reluctantly moving inch by inch away from its native stump and over to the place where I want it.

Are there then no faults at all with the winch, no limits at all to its power or my pleasure? Of course there are. All of the above. The most obvious limit is that the winch is rated at only 8,000 pounds — and even to get that you have to be pulling in perfect alignment with the direction your truck is pointed. That's why I was so careful to aim straight at the firewood truck.

The resistance of a large bull pine may well be more than the winch can cope with, especially if a couple of branches broke when the tree fell, and the stubs are jammed into the ground. I've often cut a bull pine in two before winching, and I always trim stubs.

Another problem: The little blue truck is my commuter vehicle as well as what I take into the woods, and the winch is definitely *not* a convenience when I park in town. It sits up higher than the bumpers of most cars, and protrudes beyond mine. Were I to bump into another vehicle while parking, there would almost certainly be a crunching noise as the hook of my winch made vigorous contact with the rear of the other vehicle. This makes me an amazingly cautious parker.

Winches are dangerous, too. If that cable ever snaps, I would not care to be in its path. That's one reason I'm glad the winch control is on a ten-foot cord, so that I can and do take it around to the far side of the truck when I pull anything heavy.

These are trifles. Mainly the winch is pure joy. It may even have made me a nicer person. I mean, how many people do you know who actively look for cars stuck on back roads, so they can offer free assistance?

[1991]

# Mulcho Man

THERE ARE GARDENERS WHO accept the fact of weeds calmly and even cheerfully. Coexistence is their motto.

There aren't many, though. Most of us want weeds abolished — at least in our gardens. If of methodical temperament, we do daily or weekly weed patrols. If violent, we rush to herbicides. If environmentally inclined and (we think) clever, we mulch.

I am a mulcher. Over the years I have covered the surface of my garden with most substances that lend themselves to this use, and a fair number that do not. My mulching began in disaster and has ended in glory. That makes a satisfying narrative, at least for the teller.

My mulching career began in the early summer of 1965, about two months after my wife and I were given a couple of sheep. In no way farmers at the time, we nevertheless lived in the country. And we did garden.

Sheep spend nearly all their time eating. When there isn't grass, they want hay. There is no grass in Vermont in April. So on the same chilly day that the sheep arrived, I bought twenty bales of hay. Novice that I was, it meant nothing to me that the bales were a sort of faded tan color, and had spots. It clearly meant something to the sheep, though. They took one appalled sniff at the first bale, and would never go near it again. A neighbor had to explain to me that the hay was at least two and probably three years old, had definitely been rained on in the field, and was

43

musty besides. "It'll make nice mulch hay, though," he said consolingly.

I don't like herbicides, and I was tired of weed patrol. I'd already been thinking about black plastic for several years, but was repelled by how ugly it looks, and also by that general suspicion of synthetics which characterizes a certain type of mind. Now suddenly I found myself with a great deal of natural mulch. Twenty bales of hay weigh about half a ton.

In early June, as soon as my garden rows were well up, I began shredding and fluffing and spreading baled hay. It took only eight bales, and most of a morning of hard work, to mulch the entire garden. I didn't bother to do a last hoeing, since all that purslane and quack grass were doomed anyway.

Less then a week later, the first quack grass shot up through the hay. I fluffed up ten more bales, and just about buried the garden alive. This time I succeeded. A few cunning weeds came up right in the rows, but otherwise the garden consisted of nothing but healthy plants of my choosing and long rows of moldy tan hay. Everything flourished. I was especially proud of the tomatoes. That year I was testing tomatoes — strictly for flavor; I couldn't care less about exceptional size, or absence of blemishes — and I had six plants each of six varieties. They occupied a quarter of the garden, since I knew enough to space them well apart.

Every single one of those thirty-six tomato vines grew as if someone had been out reading the story of Jack and the Beanstalk to them and they wanted to prove they could grow faster than any mere bean plant. I had to restake the whole lot of them with six-foot stakes. All honor to water-conserving, weed-killing mulch, thought I. Probably that hay is releasing valuable nutrients, too.

I couldn't help noticing, though, as June turned to July, and July to August, that my tall tomato plants were not setting a single fruit. The three unpruned vines in each set might add ten new branches (and ten new suckers) in a single night, and the pruned ones might rise another three inches toward heaven, but practically all lacked flowers, and absolutely all were fruitless. In mid-August I went whining to my neighbor.

It took Eb exactly one look to diagnose the problem. Mulch. "That might be a good way to get your vines through the winter," he said, trying to keep his face straight, "but it's hell on 'em in August. They got to have warm soil to fruit." Then he went on to explain how his grandfather used to store ice right through the summer by insulating it with hay and sawdust. I had insulated my garden.

So I demulched, and I did get a bumper crop of green tomatoes before frost came, and even a few ripe ones. And I had had my very first lesson in theory of mulch. In later years I extended my studies to such recondite matters as Wind Resistance of Chopped Oak Leaf Mulch During a Drought, and Six Serious Faults of the Common Lawn Clipping.

All this time, little did I know it, I was being led nearer and nearer to that homely and unnatural substance, black plastic. When I got there was three summers ago. I had to be away for nearly all of June, and I had decided to plant only half the garden. The other half I would cover, to keep it from reverting to sod. Once before I had covered part of the garden — and had used a beautiful canvas tarpaulin, which in only one growing season I had succeeded in turning into a large rotten rag. This time I bought a twenty-by-forty-foot piece of heavy-gauge black plastic. And then just for fun I sloped that whole section of garden slightly in toward the center, and cut a small circular hole in the plastic before laying it down. In the circle I planted three melon seeds. If I was going to have that vast weedless surface, I thought, I might as well try one more time to grow muskmelons, a crop that our soil is generally too cold for.

They say that black plastic mulch will raise soil temperature about eight degrees Fahrenheit. I am convinced my huge heavy piece raised it more. Three little melon plants shot up. By the time I got home in July, three vine systems were occupying most of the plastic. By August Tarzan could have swung through that melon patch. In September I had such a huge melon crop that I gave away delicious, rich-scented melons to people I didn't even like. They, used to the unripe, far-traveled cantaloupes commonly sold in supermarkets, actually reciprocated in one or two cases with bottles of good wine. I owe my Cabernet Sauvignon to plastic mulch. For that matter, I owe my cool-rooted peas to hay mulch, and my thriving wild blueberry bushes to pine-needle mulch.

I still think black plastic is ugly — but when it's solidly covered with a forest of melon leaves, and dotted, even clustered with large ripe melons, one doesn't really notice it much. Instead, one wonders what mulched pumpkins would do.

[1984]

# The Woodlot Adviser

♾

THERE IS NO SHORTAGE of instruction books for people who own a few acres of trees — or a few hundred, for that matter. Ever since wood stoves came back into favor in 1973, such books have been pouring off the presses. There are dozens of them.

All that I've seen take one of two forms, however. The majority are straightforward do-it-yourself. They tell you how to go out and pick the right trees to cut. They tell you how to notch and fell a chosen tree. Then they tell you what to do after it starts to fall, and—probably because you were too excited and scared to finish your backcut—instead gets hung up in another tree.

The minority instruct by indirection. These are bits of auto-biography by woodlot owners. Instead of advice, they contain stories. The owner tells how he got a tall young beech hung up in the neighboring oak, how he tried and failed to rotate it loose with his peavey, how he finally pulled it down with a rope tied to the bumper of his pickup. He tells, slightly boastfully, about the first sawlogs he ever sent to mill.

Both types assume the reader is interested in getting out there with a chainsaw and personally converting trees into firewood and/or lumber. Both tend to be quite ahistorical: wholly concerned with the immediate problems of caring for a woodlot, wholly lacking an overview.

For these reasons, a book called *Working With Your Woodland* is worth hearing about. It is aimed at the hundreds of thousands of woodlot owners who *don't* want to do their own cutting (or who may want to, but can't). It gives them more than just instructions on how to deal with foresters and loggers, though there is plenty of that. It gives them such a wealth of context that even those of us with two chainsaws, two peaveys, and twenty years' experience in the woods may want to consult it.

The three authors are three professional foresters, two in Vermont and one in Massachusetts. Among them, Mollie Beattie, Lynn Levine, and Charles Thompson seem to know practically everything there is to know about woodlots, and they write clearly besides. To be sure, they also write regionally. They focus their attention on the six New England states (sixteen million acres of woodlots, half a million owners). But most of what they say applies wherever there is hardwood forest. That is, to most of the northern United States and to a good deal of the mountainous south.

The book begins with an unexpected admission, tucked into a preface. Forest doesn't need to be managed, these three foresters say cheerfully. "It is of no benefit to the forest if 'poor' trees are removed to encourage the 'good' residuals; the quality of trees is a human judgment about their utility for lumber or some other product." And it doesn't even need to be managed in order to get the products. "Despite two centuries of bankrupt land-use and timber cutting practices, which still persist, the New England woods continue to yield lumber, fuel, [maple] sap, and game."

Then, just as the owner who loves the woods "the way they are" and hates the very idea of a tree farm is beginning to preen himself a little, they pounce. Woods don't stay "the way they are," and can't. Year by year, weather, disease, and fire change things. A high wind may flatten patches of shallow-rooted trees. A hurricane — there have been twelve major ones since white settlers came to New England — will do a messy version of clear-cutting whole stretches. Disease picks off a tree here and there. And what outside forces don't change, the forest itself does, moving slowly toward the climax state of trees that can regenerate in their own shade. (It's usually interrupted before it gets there by the next fire or hurricane.) The best management practices, they point out, simply add a measure of intelligent planning to kinds of changes that would have occurred anyway.

Now the book proper begins. After a chapter on the history of New England woodland, which includes such information as that the early settlers unintentionally doubled or tripled the population of wolves by cutting most of the overstory trees (and then spent a lot of tax money paying bounties on wolf heads), the authors turn to management techniques. First they tell the owner how to assess the potential of his or her woodland. Though I thought I knew my own woods pretty well, much in this chapter was new to me. For example, I'm used to thinking of southern exposure as desirable; after all, it gets more sun. For trees, though, a southern slope is apt to be too dry. At least in New England, trees do best on slopes that face northeast. Again, it had never occurred to me that you pay no attention whatsoever to the spindliness or thickness of the existing trees in judging the quality of a site; you go entirely by height.

From there the book moves steadily from one practical aspect to another. You learn how to choose a forester, and what kind of contract to write with one. The same with loggers. You learn exactly what to do to produce different types of wildlife habitat. Favor your wild black cherry over your red maple if you want songbirds. Leave some poplars, too. If you're an actual bird addict, have a fifteen-percent thinning cut made over your whole tract of woods. This (assuming you had dense woods to begin with) will result in three distinct layers of vegetation: a top story twenty-five feet and higher, an understory of trees and shrubs from three to twenty-five feet, and a ground layer of ferns and plants two feet and under. Each layer will support a different bird population.

The main bulk of the book, however, is a long, careful analysis of different cutting and thinning techniques. Here is where I learned most of all. Take the technique known as "release." Like anyone who has cut wood for awhile, I have known that if you take out the so-called wolf trees — the big old many-stemmed red maples, the twisty old white pines — you release the younger trees around them to grow faster. *That's* not hard to figure out. They're getting more sun. What I hadn't realized, though, was that some trees are like human beings and can benefit from improved conditions only at early growth stages. Give a malnourished two-year-old plenty of orange juice and protein, and he shoots up to be a tall adult. Wait until he's twenty-two, and he remains stunted for life. So with oaks, pines, white birches, and many other trees. Once past early youth (say, age fifteen or twenty for an oak), all the sunlight in the world won't turn them into forest giants. Had I but known it; I've wasted a good deal of time favoring sickly oaks. Ah, well, at least the even greater amount of time I've spent encouraging overshadowed sugar maples will pay off. They can benefit from a fresh shot of sunshine as late as age seventy.

The book is packed with useful information like this. It ranges from the major, such as a full discussion of girdling, to the minor and charming, such as the handiness of a metal detector if you're cutting maple sawlogs. Some long-ago farmer may have tapped the tree, and one year forgotten to remove a spout. Now, half a century later, it's deep inside, with not the faintest scar to show. The mill owner will be very angry indeed if he wrecks his sawblade on it. A couple of passes with the detector, and you'll know you're sending a safe log.

The advice isn't *that* quaint, incidentally, as I can testify from experience. Once I cut a hundred-year-old maple back behind my hayfield — it was too close to some younger, straighter maples. When I was splitting it up for firewood, I found a spout buried six inches deep. And just last year I was embarrassed to find one of my own spouts half-grown into one of my best tapping trees. I must have overlooked it (it was on the north side, where I don't always tap) six or seven years ago.

This book is not wholly faultless. Some of the sections on contracts, however useful, are a little numbing in their detail. And there is one, though only one, "fact" offered that makes you wonder just how much time these three highly literate foresters have spent actually getting up cordwood. Along with many other useful lists and tables, they include one for the man or woman out with a maul splitting logs. Elm is hard to split, they say, and no one who has gone at a two-foot elm log will disagree. Birch they call medium, and that seems right, too — provided they mean white birch. Yellow birch is up there with elm. Hemlock they say is easy. Well, maybe. But oak? Oak is hard? Nonsense. Oak is the woodsplitter's delight. Oak is pure joy. Even if they didn't know that from experience, they might have taken a tip from Robert Frost. Frost once wrote a poem — a very great one — that centers on a woodsplitting scene.

> Good blocks of oak it was I split,
> As large around as the chopping block;
> And every piece I squarely hit
> Fell splinterless as a cloven rock.

Frost was using an ax, not a maul, and still getting each piece on the first blow. Three foresters were nodding when they let that list go by.

But they don't nod often. This is a book to trust.

[1983]

51

# Gardeners' Glut

❧

ALONG ABOUT MID-AUGUST, almost every vegetable gardener faces the same old problem: what to do with all that stuff they've grown. Besides eat it, that is — which in late summer might use up a quarter of what the garden insists on yielding.

There are, of course, a number of standard solutions. You can the stuff. You freeze it. You give it to friends. Looking ahead, you resolve to have a smaller garden next year.

The standard solutions all have problems, though. Canning, for example, is a great deal of work for a very small reward. All that preparation, all those hot water baths, all the new lids to be bought for the jars — and you still get nothing better than canned string beans. In 1909, home-canned vegetables were normal winter fare, and doubtless worth the effort. At present they amount to little more than acting out the hoarder's instinct.

Freezing's quicker, though you still have to blanch the damned beans; you can't just impulsively toss them in the freezer compartment. It is also quite expensive. At least, it is the moment garden overproduction forces you to move from shoving a handful of small packages into the freezer section of your refrigerator to buying a big white chest that you will probably keep in the cellar and clomp up and down to. Quite a small garden can precipitate that move.

As for unloading your surplus on friends, it's not for nothing there are all those zucchini jokes. Giving away garden produce in late summer can be almost as hard as selling it, without even the solace of being paid. Earlier in the season it was not so; the first peas and lettuce are quite easy to give away. It's the late-bearing vines that are so relentlessly productive. If *zucchini* weren't the more picturesque word, I think there would be just as many cucumber jokes and tomato jokes.

As for planting a smaller garden, those who actually remember and do so the next spring soon discover that there is no happy medium between the purely symbolic garden (two pepper plants, a three-foot row of carrots) and one that overproduces in August. If you want anything worth eating in June and July, the late-season glut is inevitable.

Fortunately, there are some other alternatives. I begin with the assumption that among them is *not* the degenerate practice of leaving everything to rot on the vine, nor yet that experience in futility of picking everything only to transfer it some weeks later to a compost pile. Each of these is an affront to the goddess of fertility, not to mention to normal thrift.

The ideal, the gem among solutions, is to keep a pig. A piglet bought in April will be able four months later to keep up with the production of almost any garden. Pigs adore fresh vegetables, as they do most other edible substances. More important, on this healthy diet they will yield truly sumptuous pork, quite unlike the medicated stuff sold in supermarkets. I have known guests to come back for fourths when eating a crown roast from such a pig.

Obviously the pig solution is not available to everyone. Most towns and suburbs have a quite narrow prejudice (and also a couple of laws) about pigs, even though the family pig is quiet, clean, and perfectly odor-free when kept in a reasonable-sized pen. Ask Emerson. He kept one in Concord, and often took the surplus vegetables out himself.

It's large-scale hog farms that produce the smell, require the medicated feed, etc. Your individual pig is downright dainty. Daintier than people, in some cases. The two handsome pigs my wife and I raised last summer had a bathtub in their pen (we found it at the town dump), and they never missed a day's bathing. On very hot days they sometimes took four, five, even six baths, and were the picture of cool cleanliness. But of this whole side of swinish behavior, most suburban officials know nothing.

Even where no laws exist, there's usually another severe problem. No slaughterhouse exists, either. There are many reasons why this is so, not least the successful lobbying of the major meat-packers to make running a slaughterhouse so complicated and expensive that only large companies can afford to do it.

Beyond all that, of course, there are two major religions that frown on pig-keeping, no matter where you do it.

If a pig is impossible, the next-best solution is chickens. There is a widespread impression in this country that chickens are picky about what they eat, preferring only a few things like cracked corn and (when available, which in the large battery farm is never) the more succulent varieties of earthworms.

This impression is wholly false. A chicken will eat just about anything a pig will, though obviously in much smaller quantities. The only vegetable I'm aware of that chickens won't peck into is lettuce that has gone totally to seed, and hence is totally bitter. Moreover, chickens have, in terms of diet, one advantage over pigs. They love Japanese beetles. Pigs barely know such creatures exist, and have zero interest in eating them. To a gardener who not only doesn't love Japanese beetles but may actively dislike them, it can be deeply satisfying to toss a dozen or so into the chickenyard and watch the hens snap them up as hors d'oeuvres before dinner. I admit that an occasional beetle will recover in mid-toss, and fly off to settle once more on the poor helpless raspberry bushes. But not many do: hens have a good eye and a quick beak.

Many a community whose officials would turn livid at the mere thought of a family pig can stand the idea of four or five chickens, especially if there is no rooster to announce dawn. A rooster makes life more interesting for both the hens and the owners, and there are even those who think his presence leads to tastier eggs, though I am not among them. All informed persons agree that vegetable-and-bug eating hens, with or without a rooster, produce better-flavored and healthier eggs than the prisoners on the battery farm do. The difference is not so extreme as with pork, but it is perceptible to nearly all palates. Four or five chickens won't handle your surplus produce with the monumental efficiency of a half-grown pig, but they can and will consume most of it — and pass it back to you in the form of two dozen eggs a week.

What if neither a pig nor chickens is possible, and you can't even make a deal with someone in return for a share of the pork or eggs? Then the thing to do is to sit down and analyse what small number of your products are worth the trouble of preserving. If you have an apple tree, for example, you can reflect that whereas home-canned string beans are inferior to commercial frozen ones, and home-frozen ones are apt to be only slightly superior, home-made applesauce is almost invariably five times as good as even the luxury commercial brands. If you don't peel the apples first, it's prettier, too. A tender pink.

The other thing is to reflect what you can grow in a home garden that preserves itself — and that is also superior to what stores sell. Potatoes make a good example. Potatoes keep handily for six months and longer. And you can grow many succulent varieties that agribusiness never touches. From your garden you can also pull out little new potatoes the size of walnuts, and twenty minutes later enjoy them lightly steamed for supper. I know there is resistance here. Except the greasy fries (invariably of a variety called Russet Burbank) that all hamburger chains sell, Americans are eating fewer and fewer potatoes. Presumably this is from fear of growing fat. It is a groundless fear. The *grease* at Wendy's will make you fat (and don't think I'm implying that grease loses this ability at McDonald's or Burger King), but potatoes in ordinary quantities will not. Ounce for ounce, potatoes and pears tie in number of calories.

But I'm afraid these are make-do's. The only real solution is a vegetable-eating animal. Myself, if I lived in a city apartment and had even a little balcony, I might try growing vegetables on one side of it and secretly keeping two hens on the other. One hen gets lonely.

[1985]

# Smooth Operators

❧

THE WORD VERMONT ON THE label of a food product has become a marketer's dream. It's sort of like a few words in Danish (and maybe a small map with an arrow pointing to Copenhagen) on an ice cream container. People rush to buy.

In both cases, I think, the reason has to do with trust. Vermont is a little state with a reputation for being slightly old-fashioned. Denmark is a little country that Americans think of as being full of almost obsessively honest Danes. Folks like these must sell good food.

I don't know about Denmark, but in the case of Vermont the reputation is valid. The state *is* slightly old-fashioned, or at least many individual Vermonters are. They do sell honest food, mostly. Some are so old-fashioned that they put honesty above profit. For example, last fall I was at the farmers' market in St. Johnsbury one Saturday morning. It was a couple of weeks after the end of the sweetcorn season. But there was one farmer there still selling corn. Turns out he has a sidehill farm that doesn't get a frost when most places do. Knowing that, he had planted some very late corn. He had the last of it with him that day — half a pickup full — and with his monopoly he should have made a killing. He made nothing at all. Why? Well, he'd decided these last ears didn't get quite ripe, so he was simply giving them away. He wasn't even one of those quaint old types you see in Vermont photographs; he was barely middle-aged. Young enough to know he should have taken the money and run.

Just about all the food products marked *Vermont* enjoy a measure of trust, which is one reason there's currently a new brand of local mustard popping onto the market about once a week, not to mention a flood of (mostly very good) jams and pickles and hand-dipped chocolates.

But there is one product that gets trusted most of all, as well it might, being a sort of liquid embodiment of the state. I mean, of course, maple syrup. And the trust is deserved. I did once meet a somewhat shoddy producer in Windsor County (he didn't always clean his pans, and in a pinch he would use cloudy sap), but he was a rare exception. Vermont syrup is good stuff, well and honestly made.

How it gets marketed is quite another matter. There are some very sharp operators among those who sell it, or at least some very greedy ones. It pains me a little to think how they cash in on the state's reputation, as I suppose it may pain those Danes who have noticed it to think how systematically an ice cream company located in New Jersey has cashed in on Denmark's reputation.

The sharp operators include very few of the people who actually make maple syrup. In fact, I haven't met any, though I've heard about a couple. There are several thousand small producers dotted across the state who do their own marketing, mostly by mail order and in local stores. If anything, they tend to underprice themselves. There are a couple of hundred larger producers who sell at the sugarhouse, or at their own stands, and they tend to charge a bit more, as do the two sizeable companies that produce and market Vermont maple syrup.

But these prices are still reasonable. I can say that with real confidence, because I've seen the official figures compiled by the National Agricultural Statistical Service, which is one of the many arms of the U.S. Department of Agriculture. If, as they did, you take all the syrup sold in Vermont (retail, wholesale, and bulk) and make up a combined figure, the price per gallon in 1988 came to $28.90. If you do the same thing in Massachusetts, the price is $36.30. If you do it in New Hampshire, the price is $37.40. Only Maine is cheaper.

No one buys combined gallons, of course — it can't be done. What consumers actually buy, for the most part, is retail pints and quarts. In these sizes the price is naturally higher, if only because the cans cost so much. (I'll be paying $1.16 apiece for quart cans this spring, and almost as much for pints. I could get plastic jugs a little cheaper — but I hate plastic.)

Higher but still not outrageous. The average retail price that people paid for Vermont syrup last year was $10.60 for a quart and $6.40 for a pint. That's what the National Agricultural Statistical Service says. My own experience is that without looking very hard, you can find syrup at lower prices than that. For example, on the day I am writing this, you could walk into Dan and Whit's general store in Norwich, Vermont, and buy yourself a pint of Grade A Medium Amber for $4.99 or a quart for $8.99. I myself sold a few quarts for $8, last sugaring season. Sheer carelessness. If I'd noticed how fast syrup prices were rising, I'd have gone up at least a dollar.

It's when you get away from producers and from local stores that prices tend to become astronomical. Up until a few months ago, I had thought that airport gift shops (Logan Airport in Boston is a mighty competitor here) were the real winners in overpricing, closely followed by gourmet vendors like Pepperidge Farms. I've gasped at a $10 pint of syrup at Logan . . . and then I have reflected that everything is overpriced at airports, because it's a monopoly situation out there in the terminal, and because airport merchants don't think one bit like St. Johnsbury farmers. Anyway, what did I expect in Boston?

I knew what I expected in Vermont, though, and consequently I gasped a sort of triple gasp when I opened the new catalogue of Sweet Energy, the mail order house in Essex Center. Sweet Energy has built a deserved reputation for classy dried fruits: Turkish apricots, Michigan cherries, California nectarines. It has not sold much local stuff.

In the new catalogue this has changed. They've added five Vermont products, three of them maple. What caught — no, arrested — my eye was the syrup. Perfectly ordinary Grade A Medium Amber, which they had bought wholesale from Vermont Maple Orchards, one of the two big companies I mentioned. I could hardly believe the price they proposed to get. It put even Logan in the dust. They wanted $12 for a pint, $21 for a quart. Plus, of course, shipping. They'd ask another $3.95 to ship one quart. So, $24.95 delivered. That would be $100 for a gallon.

The catalogue didn't just give prices, though. There was a nice drawing of some syrup cans, and then there was an enthusiastic, I might even say lyrical, text, talking about what "we Vermonters" like.

What we like is syrup made from "vintage maples," whatever those are. We also like our syrup simmered. "Forty gallons of sap were simmered slowly to produce just one gallon of this delicious syrup," the text explained. An interesting thought. Every producer I know boils the sap just as fast as he or she possibly can; you get fancier syrup that way. Plus you end the season in April, not July.

In short, however expert they may be at mark-ups, it didn't seem as if the people at Sweet Energy knew much about maple syrup. Now that I've talked to them, it still doesn't.

They explained that a vintage maple is a mature one, and that one simmers the sap "like spaghetti sauce, on low heat, slowly, to prevent scorching." In actual fact, of course, every farmer that Vermont Maple Orchards buys from taps maples of all sizes, from forty-year-old, ten-inch-diameter trees just coming into production to grandpa trees two centuries old. And all of them boil on a big hot fire, and look to a good stream of sap coming in, and to their own skill, to avoid scorching.

The farmers who sell in bulk to Vermont Maple Orchards do

most of the work. They get between $16.50 and $20 a gallon, according to the National Agricultural Statistical Service. That is, between $4.13 and $5 a quart. Vermont Maple Orchards does the rest of the work, furnishes the can, and wholesales its quarts at $123 for a case of a dozen. That is, $10.25 each. The owners of Sweet Energy do none of the production and have more than doubled that price.

The irony is that they could drive down to Norwich, walk into Dan and Whit's, buy retail right off the shelves, and save themselves $1.26 a quart. Years ago, I met a fellow from Tennessee in Dan and Whit's, who did something like that, only more so. He had just bought every gallon of syrup in the store. As he explained to anyone who would listen, he was going to take them back to Tennessee, pour the syrup into little glass jars, and sell it for three times the price. Sort of what developers do with a farm. He was very pleased with himself. I suppose the developers are, too.

But what about the liquid embodiment of Vermont? What about that well and honestly made syrup? How does a sensible person go about getting it? Well, the Vermont Department of Agriculture publishes a list of nearly 200 maple syrup makers who welcome visits to their sugarhouses. It's conveniently divided into northern, central, and southern. All of these producers will sell syrup on the spot, and most of them will do mail-order, too. The list makes clear which do what. You can get a free copy by writing to the department at 116 State St., Montpelier, Vermont 05602.

Or you could always stop at Dan and Whit's.

[1990]

# A Crop from the Coppice

∾

IMAGINE THIS IS THE YEAR 1865. You're celebrating the end of the Civil War by taking a cruise in the Adriatic Sea. One sunny afternoon a warship comes steaming by. It's the S.S. *Immaculate Conception*, flagship of the Papal Navy. On board is the famous Italian scientist Angelo Secchi, who seems to be struggling with a small white object down in the water. It's about the size of a dove.

You can't imagine it? Too absurd? Not even Woody Allen could get away with a scene like that?

That may be, but the Boston biologist Roger Swain can — for the simple reason that he is reporting historical fact. There *was* a papal navy for several centuries. Its final warship, before the Vatican gave up temporal power, was the steam corvette *Immaculate Conception*, built in England to papal specifications in 1858. Seven years later the ship was host to a series of scientific experiments in water clarity, conducted by Professor Secchi. He used an eight-inch white disk, known to this day as a Secchi disk and still used to measure the clarity of water.

I have started with what is admittedly one of the more exotic details in Roger Swain's lively book, *Field Days*. The book itself is not exotic, and certainly not abut Vatican history. It's about common country experiences in New England: picking rocks from the garden, cutting wood, having guests for the weekend, finding a clear pond in which to swim. But in Swain's able hands, all these subjects are enlivened with a wealth of unusual background, and are seen from unusual perspectives. All are made fresh and new.

Swain is that rare thing, a good scientist who is a good writer. In fact, he is that rarer thing, a good scientist who writes with wit and dash — or, as Angelo Secchi might have said, *con brio*.

Most scientists who handle the language well tend to be solemn, lofty, even priestlike. The lay reader is acutely aware of being taken into sacred mysteries. I don't say this critically. The loftiness of a Loren Eiseley or a Lewis Thomas is a splendid and stirring thing. But it is also something that distances writer from reader as surely as the pulpit distances minister from congregation. Swain writes in a far more comradely way.

Take the opening essay, on firewood. It begins comfortably, with a reminiscence of a small boy helping his grandfather collect dead branches, break them into even lengths, and tie them in bundles. The tone is rather like Donald Hall's in *String Too Short to Be Saved*: a fond remembrance of Yankee thrift, savoring its quaintness.

Then the small boy, now grown, remarks that he and all his friends have chainsaws. To get *their* wood, they quickly and easily cut large trees. So far, an expected progression.

But Swain is just getting warmed up. What he now points out is that large trees require being split up, since sections of a two-foot log simply do not fit into a woodstove. He and most of his friends quickly tire of splitting it all by hand, and begin to price splitting machines. Their cost turns out to be high, and not just in money. There is also all the energy it takes to build them and run them. There are the numerous ruined backs people have gotten by lifting sections of two-foot log onto a woodsplitter.

And then Swain is back to gathering sticks. That is, the main part of the essay is on growing firewood by the coppice method, or what in Vermont is less elegantly called "sprout growth." Here he begins to edge toward science.

First he describes coppicing, using the homely example of a

New England red maple. If you cut one, it doesn't die. It merely puts up a dozen new shoots, all around the stump. In eight or ten years, if you leave it alone (except for one judicious pruning), it has half a dozen small trunks, each big enough to cut up for firewood, each small enough not to need splitting. Harvest them, and the cycle immediately starts over. "Some living trees have been cut down every decade for more than three centuries." Only trees of certain resilient species such as red maple, to be sure, and only (in my experience) when the stump continues to get a fair amount of sun. But a good coppicer can easily ensure that.

Now Swain enlarges his scope to include not just the question of splitting, but the whole global problem of deforestation. Briefly, two billion people — nearly half the world's population — depend on wood for heating and cooking. Vast parts of Africa, Asia, Central and South America are rapidly being denuded as the population grows. Many of the governments involved have elaborate tree-planting programs; almost none of them work. Erosion and desertification proceed briskly.

With coppicing, however, you eliminate both the need to replant and most of the erosion. The tree roots stay alive, holding the soil in place. Better yet, you get more wood — five or even ten times as much burnable wood per acre per year as if you wait for mature trees.

"A family of four needs about 0.9 tons of firewood for cooking each year," Swain writes, "and in well-managed coppice that much wood can be grown in an area sixty-five feet on a side." He's thinking of a family of four Nepalese or Costa Ricans; I reflect that the average American backyard has that much room. And for those with a little more space and higher needs: "Chestnut coppices in England have yielded 18 tons per acre per year, and the tropical legume tree *Leucaena leucocephala* has yielded 40 tons."

Finally, he comes back to his starting point, and says plainly that coppicing makes as much sense in Massachusetts as it does in

Nepal. "Grandfather, of course, must have known this all along; neatly tied bundles of firewood economize on more than string."

So the book goes, bringing a biologist's perspective to bear on one familiar subject after another. The second essay is a natural history of avocados; they have a very odd history indeed. The third's a lively study of albino flowers, such as white marigolds and white larkspur. You get the economics (gardeners will often pay extra for white flowers) and the botany both, plus a discussion of the curious fact that while human beings may prefer white flowers, the insects and the birds that do the pollinating most certainly do not.

The fourth essay is all economics, but not of the Federal Reserve Board kind. It's a cost-benefit analysis of the leaf on a deciduous tree versus the needle on an evergreen. From a tree's point of view, leaves are cheap and fast, needles slow and expensive. The leaf is a throwaway item, discarded every fall. The needle is a long-term investment with a long payback. One kind of western American pine can keep a needle photosynthesizing for up to thirty years. Never until reading this essay did I have such a feel for how trees operate.

For that matter, never until reading Swain on weekend guests did I have quite such a feeling for *them*. Good botanist that he is, he takes it for granted that they are part of the natural life of a country place, and he studies their habits just as he might those of bumblebees. With the same practical motives, too. If you want a bumblebee to pollinate your garden, it helps to remember that she'll pick blue *Delphinium nelsonii* over white every time. If you want guests to help you with chores around the place, it pays to know their preferences. Here are some of Swain's observations:

"Guests like to work outdoors, provided the weather isn't rainy, snowy, cold, dark, or buggy. They would rather reap than sow, and they are adept at ignoring weeds. If there is a choice between doing something by hand or with a machine, the machine is a clear favorite. In general, the bigger and noisier the project, the more eager guests are to help. I'm periodically sorry there aren't more uses for dynamite." Useful stuff, this.

I don't want to leave you with the impression that *Field Days* is a flawless book, because it isn't. A few of the twenty-three essays are likely to seem a little precious to the non–New England or even the non-Boston reader, such as the one on whether Harvard does well or not to strip the ivy off its buildings. (Swain knows fascinating things about ivy, though.) Many of the essays will strike readers everywhere as beginning excessively far from their subjects. The indirect lead is a Swain specialty, and sometimes he overdoes it. He'll occasionally force a metaphor, too. But though real, these are niggling flaws. *Field Days* remains a book of notable charm and grace. I think its author may be the Mozart of biologists.

[1983]

# ⁊ III ↫
# The Less Practical Farmer

# Joyful Stones

ॐ

So far in my life I've built or rebuilt about nine hundred yards of stone wall — just over half a mile. Do I say this boastfully? Of *course* I say it boastfully. Of all the physical work I have ever done, these walls are what I'm proudest of. And they are what will endure longest. Forgive another boast: They're beautiful, too. I hear that from even some rather taciturn neighbors.

But if boasting were all I was up to, there would be small reason for you to read this. I have another reason to talk stone wall. In fact, two.

The first is a generous wish to share. Wall-building is a keen pleasure. Many people don't realize that. They think it's just hard work.

Go through the woods almost anywhere in New England and you're likely to find old stone walls, built when those woods were fields and orchards. People coming across such abandoned walls are apt to comment on how incredibly hard the pioneer settlers must have worked, piling all that stone. And even to feel sorrow for all that now-wasted effort.

I want to say, "Oh, no, no, no. You've got it all wrong. This was a passion. Yes, it was a strenuous passion, for them and their oxen both. But it was also art, and it was glory." You have only to look at the perfect fitting of stone to stone in many of those old walls to know that their makers were not just getting rocks out of the fields, and not just figuring out ways to keep cattle fenced in the

69

days before barbed wire. They were giving themselves to an esthetic impulse.

Okay, grant that wall-building is a pleasure, and often a passion. Isn't it nevertheless incredibly laborious, and doesn't it require skills that few people possess? No and no. Twenty-seven years ago I believed those two things, and I had reason. I was meditating my very first wall, and two friends gave me books on how to build walls. I found both deeply depressing. One emphasized the need for digging foundations. Want a wall? First you dig a trench, and then you bury hundreds of your good stones before you get to see anything above ground.

The other book emphasized fancy details: building steps into a stone wall, making little parapets: stuff I *knew* was beyond my skill.

Both books turned out to be misleading. It may be desirable to dig a foundation for a stone wall, but it sure isn't necessary. I have laid stones right on the ground and built a wall that has now gone twenty-six and a half years without shedding one stone, or even shifting much that I can see. As to stone steps, they're seldom needed in country walls — and, anyway, after the first year or two you could make a set, just by instinct. The hands and the eye get a feel for what will work, though the mind couldn't possibly explain. This complete immediacy is one of the greatest pleasures of wall-building.

My own walls are of many kinds. Two little ones are entirely ornamental. One I built as much to frame the view out the kitchen window as anything else — and my wife liked it so much that together we built its twin, over on the far side of the driveway. There's a bigger wall that terraces the steep lawn behind the house. Half a dozen short ones that have stopped erosion in old gullies on my pasture hill. But the four biggest are what I think of as true farm walls. They march around all four sides of my best (and most visible) cow pasture, and on two and a half sides they keep the cows in without benefit of wire. These are the ones my neighbors notice and sometimes praise. Each is a hundred yards long, or longer.

## Joyful Stones

I don't want to claim too much. On three of the four sides there was existing tumbledown wall when I bought this place — and on all four sides a lot of ancient barbed wire on fallen posts. There I had only to rebuild, and maybe add a couple or three pickup loads of stone per rod, to get the wall a bit higher. The new stones I dug up in other and worse pastures, thus improving two fields by removing one stone.

But the fourth side I built from scratch, eventually with the help of an old bucket-loader on a still older tractor, and also the help of the town doctor, with whom I build wall one morning a week — his walls one Wednesday, mine the next, and so on. We don't worry too much about the old rule of putting one stone over two and then two over one. When you're using whatever comes out of the ground, you can't be that choosy. We *are* careful to get a really big, heavy stone across the full width of the wall every few feet, to bind it together. The very biggest of those stones even has a name. It's the Oxford stone, put in place with the assistance of three Oxford undergraduates who were touring America the low-budget way. I put them up for a couple of nights, and a morning of stone work was their delightful and unexpected thanks.

All very well, but what about your back, people wonder. Aren't you going to ruin it, lifting all those stones? I freely admit that there was a long period of years when I threw my back about twice a summer, working on walls. (It was worth it. People get hurt playing baseball, too.) But then I went to a physical therapist and got a set of exercises tailored to my spine, and I have not had a sore back since. What I have is low cholesterol, a flat belly, and plans for more walls.

[1990]

# Dawn Walking

∾

WHEN MY DAUGHTERS WERE YOUNG, they used to resent living on a farm. Nothing to do, each one began to complain as she got to be eleven or twelve. Nearest movie theater: thirteen miles. Nearest shopping mall: twenty miles. Nearest really *good* shopping mall: eighty-five miles.

Once during the summer when Amy — the younger girl — was twelve, she agreed to get up at dawn and take a walk with me, so I could show her that some things do happen on a farm. What I hadn't told her was that a family of wild turkeys was living in the woods next to our back pasture. They often came into it, bug hunting. Nearly every day I found feathers, and four times I had seen them.

On a cool misty August morning, a little before six, we started across the road and into the pastures. Amy could see the webs of wolf spiders glistening silver with the dew — but that didn't begin to console her for the fact that within minutes her sneaker-clad feet were wet, something that never happens in shopping malls.

But she had promised, and on we went. Fifteen minutes later we were walking beside the stone wall that separates my rocky back pasture from Ellis Paige's smooth hayfield. Mist curled slowly around us, and there was utter silence.

Amy heard the quiet warning call first, and stopped dead. "What's that, Dad?" she whispered. Then she saw. The whole flock of wild turkeys — father, mother, and eight half-grown young ones — were out in Ellis's field, catching grasshoppers. To get back to safety, they had to cross the wall and then fifty yards of open pasture before they reached a little knoll covered with pine trees.

While we stood watching, the hen turkey ran up to the wall about thirty feet in front of us, and jumped up on top. She peered in our direction, but we were motionless. On our side of the wall, there was still a barbed-wire fence to negotiate. She spread her wings, jumped again, and then glided down into the pasture. She landed running. Simultaneously, the first young one leaped onto the wall. We stood entranced while the ten turkeys came one at a time over the wall, over the wire, and gliding into the pasture, almost like planes landing on an aircraft carrier. The big tom came last.

By then we were both a little cold and damp, and we walked back to build a twig fire in the kitchen stove (it would be hot by ten o'clock) and to start getting breakfast.

That was the first of a half-dozen dawn walks we took that summer. Once we saw a mother fox — a vixen — and three cubs. Several times we just got our feet wet. Every time we had a good time together. And even now, when Amy has a car of her own and can drive to any damned mall she pleases, she still occasionally takes walks with me.

[1987]

# Silver Mornings

❧

IN RECENT WINTERS WE HAVE been getting an increasing number of silver mornings — mornings that a special kind of frost has rendered so beautiful that it hurts. Whether the increase is part of a shift in the climate or just part of some regular cycle, I have no idea.

Early on such a morning you step out, perhaps to get an armful of wood for the fire — and then you're too caught up in looking at the silver trees to do anything but stare.

Last night it was just above freezing when you went to bed, and a little misty. The snow was soft. Now the temperature has dropped twenty-five degrees, and the air is absolutely clear. Where did the mist go? It got turned into a sort of gouache, which looks as if it had been painted on every twig of every tree. Yes, and on every weedstalk, every bush, every remaining leaf on the oaks and beeches. All these things are now a delicate silver color, and just slightly fuzzy. Your eyes are not a bit dazzled, as they will be later, when the sun breaks through and all those trees and bushes sparkle with diamonds before the hoarfrost melts and drips to the ground as common water. Your eyes are merely delighted, as if you had walked out of the house and into a Japanese print or a winter painting by Childe Hassam.

The tracery in this natural painting is superb. It's not just that every twig is outlined and given a softly gleaming finish, a distinctness that it will never have again (until the next silver morn-

74

ing). It's that there are infinite small variations, such as good artists make. For example, though every tree is silvered to the last twig, the trunks stay bare. Perhaps the larger mass cools more slowly. What about the branches, large and small? The more you look, the more you see how complex this painting is. On elms the bark remains an elmish gray until the branches get very slender indeed: no more than a half-inch in diameter. Then the silvering begins — gradually. For some distance from the larger parent branch, it runs just along the upper side of the little branch. And then in the space of an inch or two the whole branch gets silvered.

Sugar maples, on the other hand, will often have frosted branches an inch or more in thickness. Hemlocks tend to have frosted upper sides to their branches right up to the trunk, no matter how big the branch has gotten.

The most beautiful sights of all, this morning, are fruit trees. They have more twigs than other trees. A crabapple tree looks right now as if it has made a halo for itself, and is living inside a cage of light. On a morning like today, I don't care if spring never comes.

[1990]

# The One-eyed Witch of Thetford

ɔ⌣

I CAN DATE PRECISELY THE moment at which I became a believer in dowsing. My wife and I needed a new water supply for the old house we had bought, and I was going to try hand-digging a well. That being quite a lot of hard work, I was naturally anxious to ply my shovel in a likely spot.

As it happened, we knew a water witch. The house we had bought was a mere thirteen miles from Dartmouth College, where I worked, but spiritually the distance seemed more like two hundred. In our new village there lived a retired dairy farmer named Milford Preston. He had one eye missing, and he walked with a limp. I suppose he was around seventy. Every older native we knew had told us he was the person to consult about wells. He could go straight to buried water, they said — just take his wand and go. Wand? Sure, that's what you call the forked stick a dowser generally uses.

We felt a little foolish about engaging a witch, both of us being products of the kind of college where you have to take science distributives and learn to think rationally. Furthermore, we were both products of city life. In each of our pasts water had been something qualified engineers provided, usually from a reservoir, not something retired farmers found by poking around with sticks. Still, I needed a reason to dig one place rather than another. We called him. He came the next day.

It took Mr. Preston about twenty minutes to find a spot where, he said, two veins of water came together, seven feet down. While he was running his forked willow stick over the spot a third time, just to be sure of the depth reading, a pickup truck pulled into our barnyard. Out stepped a young lineman from the power company, come to move the meter. He was a local man, and he saw at a glance what Mr. Preston was up to.

"Well, Milford," he said. "Havin' fun again?" The sarcasm was gentle, but perfectly clear, and Mr. Preston must have felt stung.

"It works," he said, a shade gruffly.

"Sure it works," said the lineman. "Couldn't *help* working. Just about anywhere you dig in Vermont you're going to hit water sooner or later. In this town, mostly sooner."

Mr. Preston didn't answer immediately. Instead he walked over to the grass in front of the barn, where there was a heap of sand I was using to mix cement. We followed.

"All right," he said to the lineman. "I'll go out behind the barn. No way I can see this pile from there. He" — he nodded at me — "can come with me, and make sure I don't find a way. Then you make three little piles a' that sand, and bury a quarter in one of them. If I witch it, I keep it."

"Done," said the lineman.

We had a few minutes to wait behind the barn. Mr. Preston passed the time by asking me if I planned to keep cows, now that I had bought the Townsend place. I said I didn't. The conversation languished. Then the lineman shouted to come back — and when we did, both he and my wife were looking pleased with themselves. They had not made three little piles of sand, but five. Each looked about like what you'd get if you filled a cereal dish with good bright sand, and then carefully turned it over. The piles were spaced about two feet apart.

Mr. Preston took his wand and held it in both hands so that it rode parallel with the ground. He passed it over the first pile. Not a twitch. He reached the second, and the Y of the stick dipped sharply down, just as it had when he claimed to have found the two veins of water. His expression changed not at all. He bent over, scrabbled with his fingers in the sand, found the quarter, and put it in his pocket. Then — just to be thorough, I suppose — he took the wand in both hands again, and went on to the third pile. The wand stayed perfectly level. The fourth. Nothing. The last one — and again the wand dipped down. Mr. Preston looked surprised, but said nothing. He just bent down again, scrabbled until he found the second quarter, and put it in his pocket. Then he looked at the lineman. "You ain't so tricky as you thought you was, Arnold," he said.

At the moment when Mr. Preston found the second quarter, I became a believer. There was no way he could have watched the lineman bury the two coins. Our barn is thirty feet high, and windowless in back. I was there with him the whole time. I suppose it could have been deliberate deception, a little act rehearsed in advance by Mr. Preston and the lineman. But I don't think that's at all likely, especially since it was my wife who came up with the idea of five piles and two quarters instead of three piles and one. I consequently wasn't a bit surprised when I dug my well at the place Mr. Preston told me to, and got a good flow of water at a little less than seven feet.

A year later, at a time when we knew him better and had begun to call him Milford, he told us the story of how he became a water witch. I believe that story, too. Milford came from a family many of whose members were witches. He himself completely lacked the ability, until, as a man in his forties, he was struck by lightning. That bolt, he said, made him a dowser. How? He claimed it altered his body magnetism. After he was struck, he could no longer wear a wrist watch, because within a few hours his body would magnetize it, and it would stop. But he could dowse unerringly.

That year we also learned, not from Milford, the story of how he came to be one-eyed. He was stringing barbed wire, the new kind, sometimes called hard wire, which can coil up like a spring.

78

He lost his grip on a section; it came leaping and coiling through the air, right at him. One barb penetrated an eye. People in the village believe that if he'd gone straight to the hospital, he might have saved it. But Milford was a famously soft-hearted farmer. The accident happened in midafternoon, little more than an hour before milking. It is quite uncomfortable for dairy cows not to be milked on time. Milford milked early, bleeding eye and all, and only then did he start off for the emergency room. He lost his eye.

These days I keep cows myself. I can't imagine risking an eye to spare them a couple of hours or even a whole night of discomfort. But I do feel several kinds of responsibility toward them — and certain cows also amuse and delight me. I understand his motives much better than I once did.

There is an aftermath to the story of Milford's triumph over the lineman. A couple of months later, fall classes began at Dartmouth. It was one of the years when the college provided a faculty dining room. Early in the term, I happened to sit next to a distinguished member of the physics department. Naturally I told him about Milford and the sand piles — and about his having been struck by lightning, and his theory that that celestial touch had altered his body magnetism. Then I got ready to spring my trap.

"Of course, he's just an ignorant old farmer," I said. "*I* believe his theory. But then, like most English profs, I'm exceptionally credulous. Don't you think it must really have been coincidence with the quarters and the sand piles?"

"That's possible," said the physicist. "Or he may have picked up subliminal signals from your wife or from the lineman."

"Want to bet me fifty dollars he can't do it again while you watch? Get a third person to bury the coins, so you won't know and can't send subliminal signals? We could try *ten* piles and *three* quarters."

Clearly scientific confidence is on the wane in our society. The physicist was not even tempted. "No, thanks," he said. "It might

79

also be Mr. Preston's body magnetism, in which case I'd owe you fifty dollars. There's a lot in physics we still don't understand."

"Oh, come on," I said. "Have a little faith in science. At least bet me twenty-five."

The physicist shrugged. "I'll bet you a dollar he can't do it."

I miss the old days when scientists knew they were right and the rest of us were victims of superstition. I'd been planning to split the money with Milford.

[1991]

# Baling the Village

∾

THETFORD CENTER, VERMONT, LOOKS much like any of two or three hundred other small New England villages — except for one thing. It still has a dozen tiny hayfields scattered through it. In most villages, the little behind-the-house and down-to-the-corner fields were long ago gentrified into lawns or sold off for building lots. If neither of these, then they blurred back into brush and woods.

But ours have crisp corners, and they're mowed right up to the old fencelines. They look elegant as well as pastoral.

They owe their survival mostly to one stubborn farmer in his seventies, a man named Floyd Dexter. He mows them each summer. For the ones with any decent grass he charges nothing. He takes the hay, of course; and he is well aware that with most of these toy fields, the fifty or hundred bales he gets might pay half his costs, sometimes might even cover them, but there's not a cent of profit in it. He doesn't care. It pleases him to see the village looked after.

It pleases the rest of us, too, and since many of us also like working with Floyd, his determination leads to my favorite summer ritual: the baling of the village.

The time might be the end of June, or early July. It's late in the afternoon. Yesterday, on a hot blue day, Floyd mowed Evelyn LaMontagne's two little fields. This morning, as soon as the dew was off, he raked. Now he's on his old Allis-Chalmers tractor, pulling the baler down the windrows. About every thirty seconds, a neatly tied bale of hay gets bumped out out of its long hay-making tube, and drops to the ground, as if this big noisy piece of machinery were some kind of enormous green chicken, laying bales instead of eggs.

By the time Floyd has the first five or six windrows baled, someone has come to help. Maybe it's one of Enoch Hill's sons, driving home from work in his pickup truck. Steve or Clayton or whoever instantly turns into Evelyn's, and without saying a word (you'd have to shout pretty loud to be heard over a baler) begins to gather the dropped bales into little clusters of three or four. Maybe Merry Leonard comes by about then and turns in, too. She's got her work clothes on. A couple of minutes later Steve or Clayton is driving the pickup slowly from pile to pile, and Merry is walking alongside, heaving bales in. Before Floyd has the little fields finished, the first load is built and ready to go to his barn. Later Floyd may make a bottle of beer magically appear from some inner recess of the baler (it's actually the tool compartment), and then it's time for a visit.

There's one larger field in the village: it used to be General Miller's and now it's Roger Hanlon's. Might be eight or nine acres. It has been kept manured, and it yields lots of hay. Nearly six hundred bales, last year. On the day *that* gets baled, I've known there to be as many as four trucks and seven people helping. Nobody plans it; it just happens. The local doctor, a fellow who does logging, a part-time professor (me) — we're all out there dripping sweat and happily heaving bales. Or if clouds have come darkly in, we're sweating less but working faster, because in twenty minutes it may be raining, and nobody wants to see that hay get wet.

With so many of us, the bales get snapped up as fast as they drop. Every few minutes another truck takes off for Floyd's barn. There's no actual party when the last bale has gone up the elevator — we all have other things to do — but there's a fine chance to catch up on local news. A chance also to think how nice the newly mown field looks, and to feel happy that the village is trimmed up for another year. Maybe even kept safe for another year. To feel happier still that we got to play a role. For a little while we were part of the rhythm of the season, the village, and the land.

[1986]

# Farmers' TV

☙

THERE'S A FARMER I KNOW who likes to sit in front of the big window in his kitchen. Looking out, he can see a broad field dotted with cows, and beyond that a line of wooded hills. Some mornings the field is mist-covered, like a Japanese landscape; sometimes it's dappled with meadow flowers. Sometimes two or three deer will be on the edge of the woods, standing up on their hind legs to bite apples off the old apple trees along the fence. (The cows, who have first claim but poor balance, get the lower apples — all that can be reached with four feet on the ground.)

"That window is my TV set," the farmer likes to say. "Only gets one channel. But I sure do enjoy the show."

Most farmers, however, possess a more conventional TV set. What do *they* watch . . . and enjoy? Is it any different from what other people look at? Yes and no.

To begin with a no, farmers spend very little of their time watching farm shows. They couldn't, even if they wanted to. In most parts of the country there are hardly any to watch. Take my own state of Vermont. It's officially classed as the most rural state in the country. How many farm shows are there? Two.

One's a morning show called *Farm Day*; it runs weekdays from 7:30 to 7:45. No farmer I know watches it. That's partly because they're out doing chores, but mostly because this nationally intended show is not really about farming. It centers on commodity prices.

The other is a local show produced in Burlington, Vermont. This one is called *Across the Fence*, and it's in prime time — prime time for farmers, that is. This interesting part of the day comes in two sections. Because farmers get up so early and therefore go to bed so early, anything after ten P.M. is usually wasted on them, and they have been known to go sound asleep during a commercial at 8:42. But all farmers eat lunch, known in the country as dinner. (What city people call dinner is supper in the country.) And unlike most people they eat it at home, where they can easily watch TV. Prime time on the farm is noon to one P.M., plus early evening.

*Across the Fence* runs from 12:10 to 12:30 P.M., and catches the lunch crowd. A fair number of my neighbors actually watch it, especially the first minute or so, which is community announcements, such as who is having a sugar-on-snow party where. The rest of the show is whatever the University of Vermont Extension Service wants to make it. It might be farm news, or advice on how to start plants, or it might range as far from agriculture as a program on understanding dreams.

What about real shows, such as other people watch? What about *Roseanne* and *Growing Pains* and game shows and sports and specials and movies? Well, farmers watch most of these, too, but with three big differences from the general public. One is that farm families tend to dislike violence. For example, *Murder, She Wrote* is the only popular detective show around here, and as one dairyman's wife I know says happily about it, "They don't show 'em *doing* things."

Another difference is that country people — at least on farms in northern New England — are quite moderate viewers altogether. The average adult on a farm around here watches no more than six to ten shows a week. That's partly from lack of time. Cows have to be milked seven days a week, and chores don't go away just because it's a national holiday. Few farmers sit around wondering how to fill the idle hours.

It's also a lack of choice. Cable does not often make its way across cow pastures. Morning mist, yes; cable, no. Around here, unless you happen to live on top of a hill, you get two channels, maybe three, at most four. The result is that we tend to be quite picky viewers. If we have to pinch ourselves to stay awake, we are not going to start pinching just to watch any old rerun, or some tired movie that was B-minus when new. We're going to save ourselves for the best specials, and for a handful of outstanding shows.

There are exceptions to the only-the-best rule, of course. One smart and very hardworking farmer I know devotes an hour every afternoon to soap opera. Even in planting time he is glued to the screen from one to two P.M., watching *All My Children*. "My family thinks it's a joke," he says, "but you know, sometimes they watch with me."

The third difference is that farmers almost never look at quaint shows about rural folks. We *know* all about that. What we don't know about is the urban life of the very rich, and if a farmer watches one drama every week, it's going to be something with millionaires in it. We're mainstream there.

Well, maybe there's a fourth difference, too. Farm families are probably a little more prudish than the American average. You might think we wouldn't be, exposed as we are to the intimate lives of roosters and hens, bulls and cows, etc., but we are. We don't want to see people *doing* things on the screen.

Take a conversation I had in the village store a few months ago. I'd run into a man I'll call Eben, an old retired farmer. Eben is probably the most profane person I have ever known — in twenty years, I have never heard him say a sentence more than ten words long without including at least one swear word. (I'm going to tone him down a little here.)

When I saw him, he had just installed a dish antenna, the first in our part of town. Eben has done lots of things first. So he, unlike everybody else, was getting dozens of channels. I asked him how he liked it.

"B'god, they told me I'd get a lot of new stuff," he said. "But I didn't know how *much*. Did you know there's one channel where there ain't nothin' but sex? Them folks *screw*, right on TV."

"Is that your favorite channel now, Eben?"

"Huh! I tried it. One night I thought I'll see how long they can keep it up. So I stayed up all night, and b'god they was still at it at seven in the morning. B'god, that ain't *right*."

"You did stay up," I pointed out.

"Well, b'god, I ain't goin' to again. Ain't *nothing* on none of them channels worth staying up past ten o'clock for, and least of all them sex maniacs."

The rest of us yokels might put it more temperately. But I think Eben spoke for the whole countryside.

[1985]

# Gardeners and Their Books

∾

ONE OF THE UNLIKELIEST OF ALL garden books is a science fiction novel called *The City and the Stars*. It's an early and classic work by Arthur C. Clarke, the same man who wrote *2001*. In this book he is imagining the earth about a billion years from now. There are only two surviving human cultures: one in a small pastoral country called Lys, one in a large domed city called Diaspar. People in Lys are gardeners; people in Diaspar are not.

The citizens of Diaspar have some other consolations, though, such as being immortal, and such as having telepathic machines that can instantaneously synthesize whatever they want. All they have to do is frame the thought, and the machines deliver great art, perfect tulips, tender fresh asparagus — whatever the heart desires.

Early in the novel, Alvin, a young man from high-tech Diaspar, slips out of the city and makes his way to organic Lys. One of the things that surprises him most when he gets there is to find that the Lysians go to the trouble of raising flowers. It's not that they are forced to. There are machines in Lys, too, as advanced as you might expect them to be, a billion years hence. They could perfectly well have *their* machines make tulips.

Not only that, the Lysians grow fruit. The old-fashioned way, on trees. The village where Alvin is staying is famous all over Lys for superb peaches — as well it might be: the villagers have been improving the strain for ten thousand centuries. "But when Alvin ate some choice samples, they seemed to him no better than he could have conjured up in Diaspar by no more effort than raising a finger." The book makes it clear that Alvin's taste buds are to be trusted.

So if it's not a matter of obtaining top quality, why *do* people in Lys bother to grow tulips and peaches? The answer, I think, gets at the very heart of why people garden at all. After all, artificial flowers and plastic plants (though not, I admit, synthetic fruits) have reached a pretty high level in our own culture. High enough to fool the eye. You often see people in bank lobbies or fast-food outlets surreptitiously touching the greenery to see if it's real. If it were just a matter of looking, we could all have plastic gardens right now.

But of course it isn't. A real living plant, here or in Lys, provides two things that an artificial plant does not. One is change. The bulb sprouts, grows, flowers. The lemon tree in the tub not only flowers, sometimes it actually produces lemons.

Even more important, a living plant has a will of its own. And the interplay between gardener's will and plant's will is about seven-eighths of what makes gardening interesting. You want it to flower for Christmas. It decides to flower in November. You retaliate by putting it in a cooler place and cutting down on its water. It promptly lets three leaves go limp. Chastened, you bring it back to the window and step up its water. It triumphantly proceeds to flower.

Obviously drama like this is not possible with plastic tulips, or with anything that is not alive. With the plastic you can have the results of a glowing garden, but you can't have the process of getting there. Process is another name for life itself. That's why Alvin finds Lys so much more interesting than Diaspar.

It is also why some garden books are so much more interesting than other garden books. I don't mean that some are about artificial plants and some about real, but that some are static and others have motion.

The extreme case of static garden books is the hefty volume full of gorgeous color photographs: English gardens, California gardens, the gardens of Brazil. There's no harm in such books, but neither is there much good.

Typical of such books is one someone once gave me, called simply *Gardens*. It consists of photographs of and some rather gushy text about each of thirty-three "important" gardens. Half a dozen of them belong to people with titles, two were planted by Du Ponts, and so on. Thirty-two of the thirty-three, it is fair to say, are very beautiful gardens indeed. The thirty-third is peculiar rather than beautiful, but has terrific snob appeal. Designed by a prince of the Orsini family four and a half centuries ago, it is now owned by a prince of the Borghese family. A text of about three hundred words accompanies the Orsini–Borghese photographs. The word "prince" appears five times in that small space. It appears twice more in the picture captions. Proust would love the book.

And so do I. *Gardens* has at least twenty photographs that melt the heart. There's one of a small white bridge designed by Karen Blixen (*Baroness* Blixen, that is) for her garden at Ringstedlund. Another of a topiary garden (with view of the Arno valley) in Tuscany, and a third of Lord Aberconway's long terraced garden in Wales. Each could be looked at for a full minute, and some one might want to look at again later.

But then what? The book cost a cool forty dollars. How to get more than twenty minutes worth of use out of it? Well, one might try reading all thirty-three little passages of text, and if one were sufficiently ignorant, one might learn all sorts of things, such as that Buddhism has had an effect on Japanese gardens, and that civilization in Italy is even older than the Romans, and that Countess Peggy Munster's herbaceous borders in Oxfordshire are among the best in all England.

About then it's time to put the book on the coffee table. It can earn the rest of its cost back holding cups. *Gardens* is a handsome book — and an utterly passive one. The reader is shown glimpses of thirty-three *faits accomplis*, but not one process. The book wouldn't go over in Lys at all.

At the other or active end of the spectrum is the book of directions. Most gardeners have several, and occasionally even consult them. By no means all are worth consulting — and the bigger the book the less likely it is to be useful.

The thing to avoid here is any book with the word "complete" in its title. Completeness is only sometimes a virtue. If you're interested in oriental rugs, it may be a good idea to own a book that lists all the kinds there are, and gives a history of each. But gardening books, if they give directions, should be local and limited. The main reason, of course, is that climates are also local and limited, and any universal gardening book is going to consist mainly of advice that doesn't apply.

Take another book I once unwrapped on a birthday. It's called *The Complete Book of Gardening*. A distinguished staff of garden experts wrote it, and in many ways they produced a fine book.

Unfortunately, however, it sprang from the same impulse that multinational corporations do: the impulse to make money simultaneously in as many different markets as possible. The editor was English, as were all his contributors but one, and the book was originally published in London. But the number of gardeners in Great Britain, though very large, was not large enough to satisfy the publisher. From the start, those who conceived this book planned to sell it also in the United States and Canada — and with no expensive retooling, either. The result is an approach something like that of the manual that comes with a new car. Car manufacturers, so lavish in other ways, are great economizers when it comes to manuals. They want to use the same manual for several different models. But the models are not alike. There are consequently innumerable alternate sections: tire pressure is so much if you have the two-door sedan, a quite different figure if you bought the station wagon. Skip this page if your transmission is manual. Etc.

*The Complete Book of Gardening* is considerably better edited than the average car manual, and there are no sections you have to skip. The text is carefully international — if you say "apple," you must also say "pippin"; if you're on to tulips, and discuss mainly English and Dutch cultivars, you are careful also to bring in Texas Gold. (Not one I'd recommend, even to Texans. Too gaudy.)

It must have been rather fun sitting around London editing the book. "Michael, we've been three pages without a reference to Canada." "Does anyone know if daffodils grow in Australia?" "Why don't we say something nice about Ohio when we get to horse chestnuts?" In large organizations, ingenuity tends to take the place of imagination, and there is lots of it here.

But multiple marketing creates many problems, and ingenuity cannot solve them all. Take the section on currants and gooseberries. It goes lovingly into all the marvelous kinds you can grow — as indeed people can in England. Then there's a warning that applies only to certain models: currants and gooseberries spread white pine blister rust. "For this reason, their cultivation is banned in many parts of North America, though there are no restrictions in Europe." Great. All we need to do is move to Europe. A local gardening book would not taunt us in this way.

It also wouldn't have the problems with terminology and with misinformation that so scattered a book as this inevitably has. Take the case of what the book calls stone fruits. (The ones with pits, it means.) "In most parts of the United States except in the north-central areas where winters are very harsh," the editors say blithely, "the peach is considered the easiest garden stone fruit." Yes, sure. You can see peach trees in gardens all over Boston, and growing in Central Park.

Or take the page devoted to corn. My favorite sentence in the whole book is on this page. The editors had a mighty problem with corn. You can call it corn in one sentence and maize in the next, as they do, and thus straddle your audience. But there's really no way you can tell how to raise it both in the familiar style you'd use for an American or Canadian audience and in the here's-something-exotic-but-delicious style you'd pick if addressing English gardeners. The editors opted for the latter, and most of the page is Simple Directions for Englishmen Who Want to Try Sweet Corn.

By the end of the page, the crop is ready for harvest — that is, it's time to get a few ears for dinner. As these English editors put it, and this is my favorite sentence, "Carefully pick or cut the cobs from the stems." Maybe if you were cleaning up after a raccoon you might do that.

Not all "complete" garden books are international. Some limit themselves to the horticulture of a single country, and these are preferable by far. Better yet is the garden book that concerns itself only with a single region, a state, even a county. Best of all is a book that deals with one aspect of gardening in one region. Such books won't be on best-seller lists, usually, or offered by book clubs, or pushed by discount chains, since all of these aim at wide audiences. They'll just be extremely useful. *How to Grow Stone Fruits in Lys* is about the right scope for an active garden book.

Finally, there is a class of garden books that are neither passive experiences of the great gardens type, nor active directions to be carried out on one's knees. Books in this third class are also active — they belong to Lys rather than Diaspar — but the action is mostly mental. You don't go out and plant anything; you stay inside and think.

Sometimes it's a replicative thought. The author has, right there on the page, worked his or her way toward some view of compost or of garden colors in such a masterly fashion that the reader thinks the thought, too. Sometimes it's an original thought, book-caused. The author has said things so interesting and provocative that the reader gets into a running argument (this is how one reads, or should read, Thoreau), and he discovers new thoughts of his own in the process. Normally, of course, both kinds of thoughts are prompted by the same book, and sometimes by the same page.

This is, in short, the class of literature about gardening, as opposed to instruction about gardening or passive daydreams about gardening. It is having a golden age in America right now. In the past decade alone there have been three such books published, any one of which would be cause for a country to preen itself a little.

Henry Mitchell's *The Essential Earthman* may be the best known. It's a little bit ponderous, and it's definitely anti-tree; it's also a book so brimming with confidence and wit as to be irresistible.

Allen Lacy doesn't exude quite the same confidence — he is more tentative, more ruminative. That figures, since he teaches philosophy when he's not gardening. Lacy is the master of the house plant and the small-yard plant, though he also goes as far afield as the rare, delicious, and ugly melon called Jenny Lind. Lacy is superb at kindling desire. His *Home Ground* is probably the ultimate weapon a gardener can use to convert a nongardener — say, a recalcitrant spouse. Give said spouse a copy. If he or she out of mere politeness reads two or three of the sixty-one short essays, there's an excellent chance not only that the book will be finished but that a few days later the spouse will be sneaking out to buy a hoya vine or some glory-in-the-snow.

I've saved the best for last. Eleanor Perenyi's *Green Thoughts* has everything, including snob appeal. Though Mrs. Perenyi is American-born and now lives in New England, she did her first gardening at her husband's castle in Hungary in 1939. That's not what she is writing about in *Green Thoughts*, however. There are no more than a couple of casual references to castle-gardens and life as a baroness; the rest of the book is laid in plain Connecticut, where Mrs. Perenyi has been gardening since just after World War Two.

At first glance, *Green Thoughts* seems to be a small gardening encyclopedia. It consists of a great many entries arranged alphabetically, beginning with Annuals, moving along through Daylilies, Earthworms, Endive, and ending with Woman's Place (in the garden).

But it is no such thing. Instead it is a collection of Mrs. Perenyi's thoughts on whatever gardening matters happen to interest her, coupled with many good stories of her own experience growing things, and that in turn mixed with many bits of horticultural history. There is nothing systematic here except the alphabetical order. What you hear is the voice of a brilliant woman, who is capable of being wise, funny, outrageous, learned, and contradictory, all in the same paragraph. It is typical of Mrs. Perenyi that she should be a passionately organic gardener — even one of the pioneers in that movement — and nevertheless mention calmly, "I smoke, drink coffee and alcohol, use refined sugar to make jelly, buy eggs at the store, don't like most health foods, am perfectly aware that commercially raised chickens are death but eat them anyway because no local source supplies organically raised meats."

I think that if you agreed to let me send you to one Perenyi essay, and you would judge her by that alone, I might send you to Dahlias. That begins with a little story:

> Looking at my dahlias one summer day, a friend whose taste runs to the small and impeccable said sadly, "You do like big, conspicuous flowers, don't you?" She meant vulgar, and I am used to that. It hasn't escaped me that mine is the only Wasp garden in town to contain dahlias, and not the discreet little singles, either. Some are as blowzy as half-dressed Renoir girls.

From that story she segues into the history of dahlias, one of many Aztec flowers brought back to Europe by the Spanish. And from that she glides into an essay — a truly wonderful one — on colonial Spaniards as gardeners, and on Anglo-Americans as misjudgers of colonial Spaniards as gardeners. There is not one ponderous note here, nor the faintest sense that one is being got at, or lectured on tolerance, or anything like that. (I suspect that Mrs. Perenyi would say tolerance was an overrated virtue, anyway. It's ignorance that is her target.)

From the Spaniards Mrs. Perenyi moves by an easy and natural path back to the growing of dahlias in New England, and she gives about two pages of the best gardening advice a person could ask for. Then she is ready to go on to Daylilies.

Sometimes I think Eleanor Perenyi is the best writer who ever gardened. Other times I think she is the best gardener who ever wrote. Either way she has produced a remarkable book. May it last as long as Lys.

[1984]

# A Lesson from the Cows

∾

MOST AMERICANS KNOW THE old saying: the grass is always greener on the other side of the fence. They know what it means, too. It means that whatever you haven't got is exactly what you want.

But most Americans are also at least two generations from the farm. To them that thing about grass *is* only a saying, no more connected with reality than needles in haystacks. Whereas actually it's a plain statement of fact about farm animals. All of them. Every single cow, horse, sheep, and goat I have ever known has spent much of its time trying to figure out ways to eat grass on the other side of fences. They think it grows greener over there.

Consider, for example, the lambs on my small Vermont farm. A few years ago I decided to conserve energy — my own, plus fuel for the lawnmower — by turning part of our lawn into a second sheep pasture. Just a small pasture, for two or three lambs.

The barbed wire we use for cattle won't keep sheep in, so I got two rolls of stock fencing. This is impressive stuff. It has a dozen horizontal strands, set close together at the bottom (to keep animals from creeping through, of course), and farther apart at the top. Then there's a vertical wire either every six inches or foot, depending on which kind you get. For my original sheep pasture I'd gotten wire with one-foot vertical spacing, because it's cheaper. And had soon discovered that lambs could and would wiggle their heads through.

97

So this time I got the six-inch kind. I was going to be buying very young lambs — just a month old — and I wanted to be sure I had a lamb-proof fence. What if these young ones could wiggle their whole bodies through? I have no sheepdog, and a human being isn't even nearly as fleet as a lamb. Better spend a little extra money and be sure.

For a while it worked just fine. The lambs quietly nibbled grass in their new pasture, and hardly even seemed to see the lawn and the croquet balls on the other side. Prudent me, I thought.

But when they got to be about three months old, trouble started. The black lamb, who was the biggest and boldest of the three in the lawn pasture, discovered he could ram his head through the fence, about a foot up from the ground. Then, because the hole he had rammed it through was only four and a half inches high and six inches wide, he would not be able to get it back. He'd be stuck there, bleating wildly, until some person went into the pasture, grabbed him by the shoulders, and pulled him back inside.

When this had happened about a dozen times, the other two lambs finally caught on. Caught on to what? *Not* that if you push your head through a tightly woven fence, you're likely to get caught. But that there was a way, after all, to reach that tantalizing grass on the other side. From then on it would happen at least once a day that we would hear a whole chorus of bleats from the pasture. We would go out and find all three lambs trapped with their heads through the fence, looking like three Puritans with their heads in the stocks. Eventually I had to buy a spool of soft wire and weave diagonals all around the lower part of the fence. Later still I discovered why they make wire with twelve-inch spacing. It's designed for sheep. It has just enough give so that when they get desperate enough and tug hard enough, they can pull their own heads back inside.

The next year I was late buying lambs, and I didn't want the fenced part of the lawn to get too high before they arrived. (Not

98

just for esthetic reasons, either. Tall grass gets tough, and is hard on a lamb's stomach.) A friend of mine has a big horse and a small pasture, so I blithely invited him to keep his horse at our place until the lambs arrived.

From a horse's point of view, a three-foot-high sheep fence is not tall at all, so I was not surprised that the horse spent most of the first day reaching over it to graze our lawn. True, it was more trouble for less reward than if he had eaten some of his own pasture, since inside there was succulent May grass at least four inches high, and outside there was identical grass, only much shorter. But it had the charm (so the horse thought) of being forbidden.

By nightfall there was a three-foot strip all along the edge of the lawn, neatly chewed down to the roots. That was fine with me. The horse had had an amusing day, and I would save two passes with the lawnmower the next time I cut the grass.

But I was not prepared for what happened that night. Having half an acre of lush growth waiting inside the pasture, all that horse could think about was more lawn. When we got up the next morning, the entire fenceline facing the house was bowed outward at a thirty-degree angle, where the horse had leaned powerfully against it, and the strip of cropped lawn was now four and a half feet wide. I rode him home to his owner right after breakfast, and spent the next two hours fixing my fence.

Sometimes, of course, a smart farmer can put this animal delusion to good use. My neighbor Floyd Dexter does regularly. Like all Vermont farmers, Floyd has to contend with a tricky climate. Our weather changes fast. You think you're going to make hay while the sun shines — and a half-hour later it's raining, and the hay gets spoiled. So like everybody else, Floyd gets his hay baled and under cover as fast as possible. Sometimes this means that a few bales weren't quite dry enough when they went into the hayloft, and then they develop a musty odor. Cows in the barn won't touch hay with a musty odor. Floyd knows just how to handle that. He keeps one little section of his home pasture fenced with three strands of barbed wire, instead of four, so the cows can get their heads through more easily. Then he puts the musty hay outside that section.

Confronted with tasty grass on the inside and maybe a couple of bales of good hay (what we call bright hay) in the feeder, guess what the cows do. You're right. There they are in a long row, heads through the fence, eagerly chomping musty hay. According to Floyd, who thinks cows are able to reason (I believe it, too), they reason something like this. That hay is out of reach because he doesn't want us to have it. Therefore it must be exceptionally good. So even at the risk of tearing our necks on this wire, let's spend the rest of the day trying to steal it. And they do.

It often strikes me that the eating habits of farm animals and the mating habits of human beings have a remarkable lot in common.

[1985]

# Cows and Pleasure

ॐ

THERE USED TO BE — there still is — a motto on every can of Carnation evaporated milk. This milk is "From Contented Cows," it says. I believe it. Cows are a happy lot.

It's hard to imagine a similar motto for any other domestic animal. Wool from contented sheep? Sheep are far too fretful and anxious for that. They also dislike having their wool removed. Eggs from contented chickens? Get real. Not one American chicken in fifty — probably not one in five hundred — enjoys her life much. I'm not saying some of them wouldn't if they were allowed to keep a few eggs in a nest once in a while, or take dust baths, raise chicks, scratch for bugs. But there'd still be trouble. Chickens are often mean to each other, stabbing low-ranking companions in the back with their sharp beaks. A hen-pecked chicken is not happy.

Cows are happy. Cows have a gift for it. There's a big dairy herd in Norwich, Vermont, that seems to me to typify the bovine ability to enjoy life. There are about eighty cows in this herd: black-and-white Holsteins plus a few tan Jerseys and red Ayrshires. Cows are sociable animals, and mostly the whole eighty will stay in the same part of whatever field they're in.

But they are not, like sheep, compulsively gregarious. The very word *gregarious* belongs to sheep; the Latin *grex*, *gregis* means a flock. *Egregious* means out of the flock.

With rare exceptions, sheep are never out of the flock; they'd always rather be right in the middle. But in that Norwich herd there are always egregious cows, and they have nearly always skipped off in search of pleasure.

The pasture the herd spends the most time in is bordered on one side by a plantation of red pines: tall young trees in tidy rows. On a hot afternoon, there will always be a cow or two lying half-hidden in the shady avenue between each row. I'm pretty sure they enjoy the piney smell as well as the cool. The pasture also contains a large circular pond, about 150 feet across. On any hot afternoon, there will be three or four cows in up to their knees. Then three or four more up to their bellies, and maybe one or two up to the neck. They all look blissful. Meanwhile, the main herd, now down to perhaps fifty members, is nearby, busily eating clover blossoms. Its members look pretty blissful, too.

I don't say that cows are always happy, or that no cow ever seeks out trouble. Occasionally one does. Some years ago I knew a cow who came very close to being a masochist. She liked to wander, being egregious by temperament, and in order to go at all far she had to get through an electric fence. Her system hurts me just to think about. She would walk up to the fence and bite the top wire. If the fence was on, she of course got a painful shock — and she would bellow with pain and back rapidly off. If the fence was not on, she would calmly push her way through it and set off to have adventures.

Furthermore, cows do get sick, and when they are sick they can be quite unhappy. Last year my biggest Hereford caught pneumonia in the early winter, and the vet told me to give her a shot of penicillin twice a day for five days.

The first shot was easy: she wasn't expecting it. I got no more than a reproachful look when I jabbed the needle into her rump. (And a true jab it was. Cowhide is thick. You have to push hard.)

The second was a little trickier: she couldn't quite believe I was planning to do that to her again. Right after she felt the needle, she pinned me to the side of the barn with one powerful shoulder. Not hard enough to crack a rib, or even to hurt much, just hard enough to let me know she was severely displeased. As for the third through the tenth, they were agony for both of us. I dreaded her dodges and pushes; she obviously spent most of the time between shots dreading the needle.

And yet, the very day after the shots ended, she was a happy cow, chewing her cud in a sunny angle of the barnyard, lying on half a bale of hay that I had put out to be eaten, and that she had spread out and fluffed up to make a sort of picnic blanket. She had concluded instantly and correctly, when I brought her her morning snack of grain and made no attempt at an injection, that the ordeal was over. She looked charming, legs spread out on her hay bed, and the barnyard fresh white with a six-inch fall of snow.

The happiest cow I have personally known, though, was a half-Jersey, half-Hereford steer named Eric. He enjoyed all the general pleasures of cattledom, such as being able to focus so totally on a coffee can full of grain served to him in a galvanized bucket that you could do just about anything with him while he ate. Except maybe give him penicillin shots. I never tried that. Pick up one of your son's feet while he is eating an ice cream cone, and start to take out a splinter, and you will see at once how much less totally human beings are able to concentrate on gastronomic pleasures than cows are.

But in addition to the general pleasures, Eric had some special to him. For example, at one time I kept a radio in my winter barn. Not for me to listen to while I was milking: I've never kept milk cows. For me to listen to while I was cleaning out manure, and occasionally to turn on for the cows themselves. I have neighbors who believe that cows enjoy everything but baseball, and leave a radio on twenty-four hours a day. I wouldn't do that to a warthog, let alone to my sweet-breathed, sweet-tempered, curly-haired Herefords. But I was curious to see if they liked radio at all, and every now and then I'd leave a music program on for them. Sometimes classical, sometimes rock.

It was Eric, of course, who gave me the definitive proof that cows do like to catch a few shows. One day I went out to feed hay and found the radio on — and I was pretty sure I hadn't left it on the night before. As I say, I don't believe in subjecting a captive audience to a whole night of noise.

A few days later it was on again, and this time I *knew* I hadn't left it on. Next day, again. That night I went to the barn and watched. I hid in the hayloft, from where I could see about half the ground floor of my little cowbarn, with the radio on its high shelf clearly visible to the left. I also left one light on, which usually I don't.

I expect by now you can see this coming. You know perfectly well that an eight-hundred-pound steer can't reach up with a hoof and turn knobs on an old radio. But he can reach up with his supple mouth, and Eric did. It cost me less than two hours of watching in the hayloft to see him do it.

The fact that he picked a particularly revolting talk show I hold of no consequence. Eric clearly had figured out where the noise came from, and how to make it come. But of tuning I doubt if he had even the faintest concept. After all, he was only a cow.

[1991]

# A Vermont Christmas

∾

CHRISTMAS IS SUPPOSED TO BE SNOWY in Vermont, maybe even snowbound. It was not that way last year. The weather clearly intended to let us down. After every December snowfall — there were only four, and they were small ones — it promptly rained. On Christmas Eve, in the little town of Barnet, we had cloudy skies and maybe an inch of slippery mush on the ground. The roads were bare and muddy.

There were five of us in the farmhouse on Crow Hill: two parents, a grown daughter, an eleven-year-old son, and a grand-mother. Out in the barn were only two horses and eleven hens. We had sold our sheep and planned to get new lambs in the spring. Like nearly everyone else in Barnet, we had a great deal of getting ready for Christmas still to do.

By ten o'clock on the morning of Christmas Eve we had done the regular chores and a good deal more besides. The horses were hayed and watered, the hens fed and the eggs gathered. There was a three-day supply of newly split dry stovewood on the front porch. Amy, the grown daughter, had taken Marek, the eleven-year-old, into the big town of St. Johnsbury (eight thousand people) to finish his Christmas shopping. Anne, the mother, had made and iced a giant cake. Now the true Christmas events began.

The first step was the wreath. The grandmother had had her eye for days on a big spruce tree at the edge of the woods above the house. Taking a pair of clippers (to cut small branches) and her son-in-law (to hold them for her, once cut) she sallied out. Her daughter meanwhile cut bunches of red berries from the elderberry bush in the upper pasture. Both tree and bush actually gained from the light pruning. And by eleven o'clock the grandmother had made a spruce wreath with red berries that would probably fetch twenty dollars in any city store. Mother and daughter decided jointly not to hang it on the front door. Who besides the snowplow driver would see it on the next-to-last house on the remotest road on Crow Hill? Instead they put it inside the front hall, where everybody stopping to put boots on or take them off would see it.

Next came the tree. The mother had had her eye on *that* for a whole year. It was a furry young spruce that had come up in a corner of the lower pasture. Sooner or later the father would take it down anyway, since what you want in a pasture is grass, not evergreens. Right now it was a graceful young tree just about the height of the mother herself — that is, five feet five inches.

For a Christmas tree, the whole family goes out. Marek carried the bucksaw and cut the tree; his parents carried it back between them. Three dogs formed an escort: the two family dogs and the dog from the last house on the road, who found life more interesting down here with the horses and the chickens and the boy.

We hardly had the tree up when two things happened simultaneously. First, the already dark sky grew darker, and it began to snow. And then the phone rang for Marek. The call was from two cousins known to him as Sam 'n' Eli. They live a thousand miles away with their mother, but spend their vacations in Barnet. Their father lives two miles up the road with his second wife, two stepdaughters, and a baby. That place is a sheep farm, too.

Marek, who had thought he would probably die unless he put all the really important decorations on the tree himself, now realized that a far likelier cause of death would be if he didn't see Sam 'n' Eli immediately. Amy drove him over through the now fast-whirling snow. And decided, since she was out anyway, to go once more into St. Johnsbury (it's only five miles), where there are stores and public Christmas decorations and even a small amount of city grime.

The rest of us went on decorating the tree, occasionally sneaking off to wrap another package. Our plan was to finish the tree, take a walk in the woods to enjoy the new snow, have an early supper, and then go to the seven P.M. carol service at the Congregational church in Lower Waterford. Midnight services sound wonderful, but in farm country seven P.M. draws a much better crowd.

The plan did not work out, because soon the snow thickened. The first truly heavy fall of the year came sliding down. One result was that Amy's car did not make it back from St. Johnsbury. Crow Hill is very steep, and its roads are full of curves. With three inches of wet snow, you almost inevitably slip into the ditch if you have a two-wheel drive car.

Amy had a good walk home in sneakers. Her father took the little farm truck with the winch and winched her out, but they made no effort to bring her car back up to the farm. They left it in a neighbor's level pasture, down by the brook called the Water Andric. Everything was now pure white, and the road the purest and whitest of all. No car had been up Crow Hill for hours, and even the tracks of my little truck soon faded. In places where there were fields beside the road, but no fence, it was beginning to be hard to tell where the road *was*. Not a night to take grandmothers on back roads to Lower Waterford.

It turned out to be a good thing we didn't go. Because about eight P.M. there was suddenly singing outside, and the light of candles. The five cousins from up the road and their parents were standing outside in the fast-falling snow. Everyone but the baby held a candle, and all but the baby were singing "O Little Town of Bethlehem." We hadn't heard them come, because there is a very sharp uphill turn where the end of our driveway meets the town road, and even though they had come in a four-wheel Bronco, they had gotten stuck. Never mind that now. We had them in for hot cider and more carols.

Then it was too beautiful to stay in. We found more candles. Eleven people and three dogs walked through the silent snow to the last house on the road — the grandmother stayed home —and sang "Good King Wenceslaus." The eleven-year-old, who had been allowed to open one present early, and who had headed unerringly for his new bugle (he feels packages, and we suspect him of having a hidden x-ray machine) blew a sort of fanfare. It didn't sound too bad in the soft snow. Then we got the farm truck and winched the cousins' Bronco back onto the glistening road. Tomorrow would be as white as Christmas can get.

[1989]

# ～ IV ～
# Finding New England

# The Factory in the Woods

❧

IN THE NORTHWESTERN CORNER of Connecticut, there is a pretty little town called Colebrook. The landscape is serene and pastoral. The two main villages, Colebrook Center and North Colebrook, have both recently become National Historic Districts.

About fifty years ago, a small boy spent many summer days exploring the woods of North Colebrook, near his uncle's farm. One afternoon he happened on a many-windowed old building, deep in the woods. (At least that was how it struck his nine-year-old mind. Actually the building stood about twenty yards from an old town road. But now there was a thicket of young trees where once the entrance drive had gone.)

It didn't feel like an abandoned house. Looking back, the boy would remember the absence of lilacs in the dooryard, and the fact that no one side seemed clearly to be the front.

That day, however, he spent little time trying to figure out what the structure must have been. He was too interested in the gleam of the afternoon sun on the old small-paned windows. Many panes, of course, were broken. But even more were not — it was as if they had been saved specially for him. Without making anything that could be called a conscious decision, he looked among the roots of the birches and pines for a stone of suitable size. New England soil being what it is, he quickly found one. He threw it. With a fine splintering crash, a pane of glass broke.

This was too keen a pleasure not to repeat, and he went to look for another rock. He threw again, and another pane went tinkling in. Soon he shifted to a better source of missiles: a pile of rosy old bricks, mostly fragmented, that he found on the north side of the building. Pieces of brick throw well. Before he started back to his uncle's house, he had broken every remaining pane on the first floor, and most on the second. When he got home to supper, he said nothing about the adventure to his aunt and uncle. Long before the age of nine, experience had taught him that anything that much fun was likely to be disapproved of by adults.

Years later, when he was a relatively sophisticated college student, he dated a girl in Colebrook Center whose mother was trying to assemble enough panes of wavy old glass to reglaze all the windows of a colonial house she was restoring. Listening to the mother, he felt almost awed by how much history he had been able to smash in a single afternoon. By then he also knew what history it was. He knew that the building he had found was the old cheese factory in North Colebrook, one of the thousands of industrial ruins that were and still are scattered across New England. The mother's passion affected him. If given a chance, he would retroactively have saved those windows.

But another dozen years had to pass before he began to think in terms of beauty as well as of history. Now a teacher, husband, and father, he had come to own an old house himself: an 1820 Federal brick farmhouse in eastern Vermont. He and his wife had bought it cheap because the roof had been about to fall in, and because there was no water, and because the attached barns were an unholy mess.

The front and both ends of the house had been modernized sometime around 1900. Among other things, the original windows had been replaced with Victorian two-over-twos — easy to clean and quite homely. But whoever did the job had economized on the back. There the original small-paned windows remained: nine-over-sixes, wavy glass with an occasional tiny air bubble.

Each pane was different. Those windows took a lot of scraping and puttying, and before he had finished, the grown man fell in love with old window glass. It now struck him that he might have destroyed more beauty by throwing bricks at the cheese factory than he would have by, say, chopping down the apple trees in his uncle's orchard. Apple trees grow again.

In no way do I blame myself for taking more than twenty years to come to see beauty in the North Colebrook cheese factory. Windows apart, it can never have been a specially handsome building. Anyway, it was a *factory*, set down in a pastoral landscape, and I was raised in the tradition of the Romantic poets. In this tradition, nature is a healing force, and industry is a disease, a kind of blight. Industry attacks a green valley the way mycelium attacks a green leaf. In extreme cases it will leave the valley black.

The opposition can be put in religious terms as well as medical, and it often was. The most famous single reference to industry in the poetry of the Romantics was made by William Blake. And what did he say? He said that "dark satanic mills" were taking over England's green and pleasant land. God is a shepherd, as we know from the Twenty-third Psalm. The devil turns out to be an engineer.

The thought is one that precedes the Romantics. Milton had it, for example. In his story, God designed that green and pleasant place, the Garden of Eden. Satan meanwhile set up smelting plants in hell, and went into the business of producing iron, copper, and tin. He also built the first firearms plant. Samuel Colt's factory in Hartford, Connecticut, came much later.

The thought is still with us now. You find it, for example, in Tolkien's *Lord of the Rings*, where Saruman's fortress-factory of Isengard is a type of hell, and Saruman himself a satanic figure, master of many furnaces. Isengard (the name seems to mean Iron Shield) is eventually conquered and redeemed by an assault of the trees, by ents and huorns, much as the North Colebrook cheese factory was surrounded and finally conquered by birches and pines.

Milton, Blake, and Tolkien were not wholly wrong, either. Factories and mines do frequently blight landscapes. There is a blighted landscape not three miles from where I live: a vast ruined slope covered with tailings from the Strafford copper mine. The mine closed in 1954; the slope stays poisoned, and will for many years to come.

But not all mills are satanic, and I think especially few of them may be in New England, where from the very beginning there has been a symbiosis between the pastoral and the mechanical. That is, we have always had what I think is called a mixed economy. The early farmers produced and marketed hand-made nails in their spare time: they were metal-workers as well as shepherds of flocks. The early mill-owners were apt to keep (and sometimes personally milk) a family cow, just as an early philosopher like Emerson raised (and sometimes personally fed) an annual pig, and an early novelist like Hawthorne personally tended a large vegetable garden and personally split wood.

The result is that we have always had what could be called a mixed landscape. Forests and fields and factories have coexisted — not always happily, but often. And it is worth remembering that though the forests were here before the first Indian, let alone the first white person, set foot in what is now New England, and hence can be called natural, the fields and the factories are both manmade. One is undoubtedly more artificial than the other, but both are, in the literal sense of the word, manufactured, since the "facture" part means *to make*, and the "manu" part means *hand*. Handmade fields and handmade factories in early New England: both are apt to have stone walls.

The mixed landscape of my own town in Vermont makes a good example. Thetford has historically been farming country — better farmland than Colebrook, because fewer rocks. Even now, when the almost insane policies of the U.S. Department of Agriculture, plus the widespread decision of teenagers to be consistent and wash down their junk food with junk beverages, are rapidly destroying dairy farms, even now Thetford farmers ship much milk. That means many cows in town. And that in turn means many beautiful pastures, because cows are wonderful keepers of fields. They can produce greensward on which the grass is so neatly cropped that the suburban lawn was developed in conscious imitation. They can clip around rocks and up to walls far more deftly than any human with a string trimmer. They will keep all trees (except evergreens) pruned up to a uniform height — namely the five feet that is a cow's convenient reach when she has her head raised and her tongue out at comfortable leaf-flicking distance. As I write, the thirty-two acres of pasture on my own farm are in just such condition, kept so by the twelve Jerseys and Holsteins who spent the summer here and the five Herefords who are year-round residents.

But the seal of the town of Thetford, which is rather elaborate, shows a tree-bordered lake, a good-sized factory beside a river, and a dairy farm with twin silos poking up above the barn. Underneath are three legends: Scenic Beauty — Industry — Agriculture.

Go a hundred feet east from the easternmost edge of my farm, and you will come to that river. You will not see any factories. The one on the seal exists, and still operates, but it's four miles upstream, on the far edge of town. What you will see is the covered bridge that takes our road, once called Mill Street, into the village of Thetford Center. Just below that you will see a partly ruined dam, and below that the Ompompanoosuc River cascading down a long series of rapids. The dam is concrete and fairly modern. A local farmer named Charles Vaughan built it in 1916 and thus brought electricity to the village.

Keep looking. There are many birch trees and young elms (this is a beautiful place), and in the summer not all the old foundations are easy to spot. But they're there. Look over at the far bank of the little river, and you will gradually notice one massive stone foundation after another. A hundred and thirty years ago there were five mills in a row along the river here, and there were three dams, one below the other, to supply them with waterpower. Thetford Center was a mill village, but it was neither dark nor satanic.

Industry came to the village around 1806, when a couple of local men set up a carding and cloth-dressing mill. Over the next half-century, more different kinds of factories lined up their waterwheels next to it than you might think possible. A carriage factory sprang up, and a factory that made window sashes and shutters. (You can still see shutters of its distinctive design all over town, including on my house.) Also a potato-starch factory, a scythe and axe factory (with a one-person workforce), a musical instrument factory, an axle-tree maker, and a cabinet shop. A piece of furniture made there is now in the Metropolitan Museum in New York.

Most of these "factories" were tiny — if they *had* been satanic, they would have been run by imps, not full-grown devils — and most of them lasted for only ten or fifteen years. Then the building and the wheel and the water rights would pass to someone else.

But wars, which invariably produce war profiteers, are a great stimulus to industry. During the Civil War, and for a decade or two after it, little Thetford Center had several large manufacturing plants. Well, middle-sized, anyway. One, called the Noosuc Mill, was about half a mile downriver from the covered bridge. It employed about twenty-five people, and it made a thick, tough, yellowish paper known as strawboard, and also the binder's board used for hardcover books. A few years ago, when my wife had our kitchen remodeled, there turned out to be a double layer of that heavy yellow paper under the kitchen floor as insulation. Not too surprising, I suppose, because our house was once owned by Horace Brown, a native of Thetford Center who returned from the Civil War as an army captain. His first move was to buy the Noosuc Mill, and he kept it until he started a shoe factory, still farther downstream. One would expect him to insulate his own house with his own strawboard. What you might not expect is that this small-time industrial magnate would have a second barn built onto the end of his house, complete with inside silo for storing winter cattle feed. But he did.

Finally, nearly a mile below the bridge, was the woollen mill, which ran from late in the Civil War until about 1880, and which in its best days had about fifty employees. It must have been a stunning sight to see all those mills running at once, all those waterwheels turning, and the great leather belts taking the power from the wheelshafts to the machinery. The falls may have been more beautiful then than they are now, when there are only the halfbroken dam and the half-hidden foundations of some of the mills.

Even the great villainous industry of this part of Vermont has left beauty behind it. Some six or seven miles from Captain Brown's house is another and much older copper mine. This one had its beginning back in 1820, when people living along Copperfield Brook in the town of Vershire organized what was called the Farmers' Company. The farmers dug a little ore by hand. They also "erected a rude smelting furnace," as a man named Hamilton Child put it in 1888. They even made a little money.

But they had neither the capital nor the technology to do large-scale mining. Serious operations didn't begin until six New York City investors bought the mineral rights in 1853 and set up business as the Vermont Copper Mining Company. They put in some serious furnaces, and by the end of the Civil War around 150 people were working at the mine and the adjacent smelter. Then, just about the time Captain Brown came home from the Civil War to take over the strawboard plant, a still richer investor from New Jersey named Smith Ely took over what soon became known as the Ely Mine. (And the little village of Copperfield became the growing new village of Ely.) Where there had been three farmhouses in 1850, there were now a hundred families living, plus two churches and a dance hall.

Smith Ely thought big. The miners, all four hundred of them, worked by candlelight — one candle per miner. But the smelting plant went modern. By the late 1870s he had a refinery seven hundred feet long and sixty-two feet wide. He had twenty-four furnaces and seventy desulfurizing ovens. He was making copper ninety-five percent pure, where the early farmers thought they had done well to get the proportion of copper up to twelve or fourteen percent before they shipped their product off to more sophisticated refineries on the coast.

Smith Ely had also produced a miniature version of contemporary acid rain. Twenty-four furnaces make a lot of smoke. Smoke of his kind contains a lot of sulfur dioxide. His first achievement was to produce a defoliation of the hillsides along Copperfield Brook as thorough and as devastating as that which later Americans produced in Vietnam. Next to go was farming up and down the valley, as the grass died. About then a new kind of Farmers' Company formed; and since there was no Environmental Protection Agency to complain to, the farmers complained directly to the mine officials. They may even have waved pitchforks in a menacing fashion. And the officers of the Vermont Copper Mining Company responded just exactly as the EPA would have made them a century later. They figured out a way to spread the pollution around, so that people in the valley would get a lot less, and everyone for miles around would get a little bit more.

The technology didn't exist then to put up the kind of EPA-mandated giant smokestack that now distributes industrial pollution so freely across the United States and even around the world; but Vermont is hilly country, and an early version of pollution-sharing *was* possible. The Vermont Copper Mining Company dug a trench all the way up the side of a small mountain behind the smelting works. Today you'd probably put a non-corroding pipeline up such a trench. They didn't have the technology for that, either. Instead, with men and oxen they brought stones, and they made the trench into a walled tunnel. It rises five hundred feet, from where the smelter used to be clear up to the top of the hill, and it is nearly half a mile long. All that way they capped it with huge flat rocks — rocks as big as double beds, some of them, and four to six inches thick. These were fitted so tightly as to be smoke-proof. The smoke was forced up to the summit, where it caught the wind and rode out across eastern Vermont, to begin its descent into other valleys.

Partly because there was never a railroad up to Copperfield, so that the coal for all the furnaces had to come nine miles by wagon and the smelted copper had to leave the same way, the Ely Mine failed in the 1880s. Easier mines to work were being discovered, first in Michigan and then still farther west. But there is no ghost town, as there might be in Colorado. Dry climates preserve industrial sites indefinitely; tropical jungles swallow them up almost at once. Vermont is somewhere in between.

Today there are no traces of the seven-hundred-foot smelting plant (or the dance hall, either), except on a few acres of level ground so poisoned that trees still can't grow. There you can sometimes pick up a fragment of an imported Scottish fire brick, packed into the silty yellow rubble. Just above that spot, however, and across the brook, nature is back. The once-desolate hillsides are handsome with oak and birch. Isengard is fallen.

But not entirely, not yet. The stone tunnel up the hillside is still there, now lost in trees. It is one of the most beautiful ruins I know. Some of the capstones have fallen in, and a few at the lower end are missing, presumably hauled away by people who know a beautiful slab when they see one. Where the tunnel is thus uncovered, sometimes a young tree is growing right inside it. At these roofless spots you can see the inner stonework on the two sides of the tunnel. It is better drystone wall than I can build, though I have been repairing old walls and building new ones on Captain Brown's farm for a quarter of a century.

When I first saw that solemn ruin in the woods, I had no idea what its function had been. None of the select few people I have

taken to see it have guessed, either. They have imagined miners —
very short miners — running down it in the winter, with wheel-
barrow loads of ore. They have imagined water rushing down a
sluice — though once we reach the top of the little mountain and
there is no brook up there where the tunnel ends, or so much as a
wet spot, they've had to give *that* theory up. In the end, they've
had to be told, as I was.

But not one has failed to be impressed, as one might be by a
pyramid. The final legacy of Copperfield Village has been an
addition to the natural beauty of the region, a human accent mark
on the hill.

Industry comes and goes in New England. Right now more is
coming than going, at least in the part where I live. At this very
minute there is a proposal to rebuild the dam below the covered
bridge in Thetford Center, and resume the generation of electricity. There is also resistance to the proposal, both because a lot of
trees would be cut down and a small powerhouse built, and
because a historic site would be disturbed. (The irony, of course,
is that it's historic for waterwheels and other forms of power
generation.)

I see no assurance that present or future waves of factory-
building will leave such handsome remains behind as former ones
have. The people who built back then had the advantage of natural
materials, which generally age well. It's hard to go wrong when
your ruin is of stone, or rosy old brick, or weatherbeaten clap-
boards. But most modern factories start with basically ugly materials, and they age quite badly. If I imagine a boy giant tossing
boulders at a modern industrial plant, I see a ruin of concrete and
plastic that would simply be a blight on our green and pleasant
land.

Actually, I don't even have to imagine. I know what a concrete
and plastic ruin looks like. What are filling stations made of?
Concrete, plastic, blacktop, and sheet metal. I have seen half a
dozen that one oil company or another has built, found insuffi-

ciently profitable, and abandoned. They are not aesthetically pleasing. They never *will* be aesthetically pleasing.

But here I go too far. How can I know they never will be? It is notoriously hard to judge the artifacts of one's own time. I have seen photographs of Copperfield Village in its heyday, and that was an ugly sight, too. If I had lived then, I think I would have said that corner of Vershire was ruined, probably forever. I think I would not have imagined people coming a century later to stare in awe at the smelter chimney.

Unless we manage to kill off trees and grass altogether (in which case we'll presumably kill ourselves off, too), it may be that the alternating cycles of forest, farm, and factory will keep on making the New England landscape richer and richer for a thousand years to come. It's a nice thought, anyway.

[1988]

# The Soul of New England

cᔢ

RECENTLY I LEFT MY FARM for a week. I flew from Vermont down to Boston in a little plane and then from Boston out to California in a big plane. I was going to a conference at that exurb-of-Los-Angeles branch of the University of California called Riverside. And never having been in southern California before, I had come a day early. I wanted to see the landscape. I wanted to do it the only way worth doing: on foot.

As it turned out, the landscape made me nervous. There were plenty of individual elements I loved, such as the double rank of bottle brush trees marching up the avenue at the main entrance to UC Riverside. But the countryside as a whole was too naked for my taste. All those bare, lion-colored hills and all that sweep of sky left me feeling exposed and vulnerable — a little bit like how a mouse would feel (I imagine) if you put it out in the middle of a basketball court. A New England mouse, anyway.

The evening of that first day I devoted to looking at the city of Riverside itself. It's a small city by California standards but quite a big one by the standards of New England. It has 226,000 inhabitants, which makes it more than twice as big as anything in Vermont, New Hampshire, *or* Maine. In all New England, only Boston exceeds it.

I was staying in a motel out by the university, and what I did was to stroll downtown just before dark. Some stroll! In the first place, downtown proved to be elusive. I'm not entirely con-

vinced Riverside has one, at least not in the eastern sense of a
thronged center where building density is much greater than
elsewhere, where you can't easily park, where things are *old*. In
the second place I remained tense. It was the same mouse-feeling
I'd had out on the bare hills. Only this time the streets were the
cause.

I was walking down a broad avenue which crossed side streets at
regular intervals. Every time this happened, I went into a state of
mild panic — that is, I panicked once a block.

Don't scorn me entirely. Those were formidable side streets,
like nothing I had ever seen before. Each had six traffic lanes and
two parking lanes, for a total of eight. At home in Vermont not
even the two interstate highways are that wide. I'm not sure the
Connecticut River is.

I had to force myself to cross. After the first couple I no longer
had any fear of being squashed out in the middle by some crazy
California driver. California drivers proved not to be crazy, instead
quite gentle. No one shot round a corner with squealing tires or
threatened me by speeding up slightly, as drivers sometimes do in
Boston. And as they even do in West Lebanon, New Hampshire,
for that matter, in front of the shopping malls.

My fear — I knew it at the time — was quite irrational. Simply,
I felt too far from the nearest tree. Or, rather, this being a city, too
far from the nearest doorway. Even when I had made it across a
street, I was still a long way from shelter. These eight-laners were
not bordered by comforting buildings. They were bordered by
emptiness. Every laundromat and photo shop had been set back at
least a hundred feet, and the intervening space was generally
paved. I couldn't even have burrowed into the soil, had a helicop-
ter come thumping down to catch an unwary visitor.

That trip taught me a lot about California, but it taught me even
more about New England. Opposites may or may not attract;
they do clarify each other. And northern New England and

southern California must be about as opposite as any two parts of the United States can get.

They have things in common, of course, both being part of American culture. Teenagers in East Topsham, Vermont, listen to the same American Top Forty songs as teenagers in Redondo Beach, and (except all winter) they wear the same gaudy sneakers. They don't eat the same too-rapid food as much, but that's only because they have to go all the way into Barre to get it. Fast food is not available in Topsham. Church suppers are.

So it goes through the whole spectrum, from theology to garbage collection. There are Hindu ashrams and Buddhist monasteries in New England as well as in Los Angeles. Compactor trucks in both places make the same unearthly whine as they swallow the same plastic garbage. Even scenically the two regions share much, from identical phone poles to interchangeable road signs to similar-looking storage buildings slapped together of cement blocks and then painted pale green. (Somehow I find them even uglier in New England than in California, probably because I have a clearer image in my mind of what a New England building ought to look like.)

But if there are many likenesses, there are even more oppositions. As I came back on the jumbo jet to Boston and then on the little plane to Vermont (nineteen passengers, no cabin attendants), I kept thinking about them. It seemed to me that I saw the true nature of New England more clearly than ever before.

Let me start with the landscape, then advance briefly to the people, and finally I'll say a cautious word about the soul of this region. Not all regions have souls, at least not living ones, but New England does.

The central truth about our landscape is that it's introverted. It's curled and coiled and full of turns and corners. Not open, not public; private and reserved. Most of the best views are little and hidden. It was only after I started doing contract mowing of hayfields around town that I got behind people's houses and saw vista after vista that you'd never guess from the public roads. We like secrets.

Did I call our roads public? They mostly aren't, other than in the legal sense. They are narrow, except for a few monsters curving around Boston and Hartford. Even when country roads are bordered by fields, there's apt to be a line of trees and brush that effectively secludes the traveler. Or if they do offer a view, it's small and domestic. Even a New England interstate can offer private views. In fact, the road I'd pick to be emblematic of the region would not be one of the thousands of little dirt roads curling and coiling all over the six states, including Rhode Island. They are indeed emblematic, but perhaps more of the past than of the future.

What I would pick would be Interstate 91, the stretch beginning at mile 112 in Vermont, going north and coming over the crest of the high ridge just beyond Wells River. That section doesn't look like an interstate at all. What you see in the valley below is a pastoral scene with what appear to be two separate two-lane roads running parallel, a hundred yards apart. What is actually a small rest area gives the impression of being a side road, curving off to the right. In short, the whole road project has been domesticated, and instead of cutting the land apart it stitches things together. And that is an emblem of how our humanmade landscape, at its best, interacts with what was originally here. I greatly prefer it to big faces on Mt. Rushmore, or the six- and eight-lane concrete strips that press down so hard on the poor suffering but still beautiful meadowlands of northern New Jersey.

Let me take my own farm as an example of how the land is arranged. If you were to drive by it on the town road, you'd notice a fairly handsome old brick house, with a big red double barn attached to the western end. Across the road you'd see a few acres of cow pasture, fenced partly with barbed wire and partly with very handsome stone walls. (You'd better think them handsome. I built them.)

That's all you'd see, but it's hardly all there is. Behind the house, completely invisible except to one set of neighbors across the valley, is my best hayfield — which is also the best kids' sledding. I almost lost a friend who couldn't resist observing, every time he came to visit, what a fine three-hole golf course that field would make.

Across the road there is a great deal more. Behind the field you can see from the road, three other fields curl around a steep hill, and a steep pasture goes up it. To walk from one field to the next — *this* with its pine-covered knoll where the cows like to hide when they are about to calve, *that* with its oak tree older than the place, and its high cliff boundary — is like walking from one stage set to the next. Everything is so up and down, and so deeply wooded where it isn't pasture, that my little ninety acres offers a dozen places to get lost. Even now I don't know every inch. It was only six years ago — nineteen years after I bought the place — that I stumbled on the fort. It's a giant rock that some glacier left: the length of a school bus, but higher and wider. Centuries ago frost split it lengthwise, and then split one of the side pieces as well, so that there is a T-shaped passage right through the great rock. A hundred-year-old yellow birch grows in that passage; dense woods surround the entire rock and conceal it.

What caught my eye as I pushed past the last bull pine was the fortification. At some point long ago children rocked up each of the three entrances to about waist height, and at least one of those children really knew how to lay up stone. It is beautiful work. An average of one new person a year sees it. I have begun to worry that I am showing it off too much.

That rock is not the sacred place on my farm; the huge old oak marks that. But it may yet become sacred — in fact, the whole farm seems to be in the process. Which is one reason why I have taken steps to keep it a farm.

There are sacred places on nearly every piece of land in town, except maybe our one small commercial zone. And I would claim that the deepest truth about New England as a place is that, with the exception of some Indian reservations, it contains a higher proportion of sacred land than any other part of the United States. By "sacred" I obviously don't mean formally consecrated to a religious purpose — though there's a fair amount of that, too, around convents and monasteries in Massachusetts, not to mention around the lamasery thirty miles north of here. I simply mean land valued other than commercially — land for which the highest use (as tax appraisers quaintly say) is not discovered by finding what will bring the biggest cash return, but by finding what will make the land most beautiful, most productive, or most healthy, and sometimes all three together. And, yes, when I make that claim, I speak in full awareness of the million acres of the Adirondack Preserve in New York, and the Amish country in Pennsylvania, and all those Civil War battlefields in Virginia, and Yosemite, and . . .

I'll offer just one piece of evidence for my claim — but what a piece! Nine years ago, when I was first looking for ways to protect my farm from high uses, I did some investigation of private land trusts: organizations dedicated to land preservation. At that moment there were somewhat under five hundred of them scattered across the United States. Some states had one or two; some had none. Connecticut had eighty-two and Massachusetts sixty. No state outside New England came even close to these figures.

The people of New England are a good deal harder to generalize about than the land. We are a seacoast people and a lakeshore people, as well as land-lovers. There are sacred coves, too. My wife grew up on one, and even now she wishes it were possible to hear foghorns on our farm. We may not have any seriously large cities except Boston, but we have hundreds of mill towns, some grimy, some not. We are partly French-Canadian, partly old Yankee, partly Italian, partly twenty other things. There are Mashpee Indians on Cape Cod, and there is a jai alai fronton in Hartford. There is now one county in Vermont that has an actual majority of upscale newcomers, and in that county a term like "Sunday brunch" is heard more frequently than a term like "church supper." I believe they have hot tubs, too.

But climate and topography do play a role in determining human character. And the example set by native Vermonters does seem to have an effect. That same county also has an enormous number of houses heated by woodstoves, and the sale of chainsaws to newcomers is brisk. Despite the vast changes of the last twenty years, I think it is still accurate to say that the basic New England characteristic is a kind of humorous stoicism. You *expect* it to snow just before you have to drive a hundred miles, and to be sleeting when you have a day off to ski. You are not surprised when your pipes freeze, and you probably have a wry comment to make. I love one I heard last fall, made by a woman in New Hampshire. She herself lives in a small city (about one-eighteenth the size of Riverside), but she has a daughter in the country who runs a cider press. She had filled her car with apples at that press, to take to another daughter in town, who was going to make applesauce. Before she could deliver them, a storm came up, and blew over a fifty-foot tree in her yard, on top of car and apples both. There are a good many things one might think to say at such a moment. "It sure put a cleat in my car," she said. "I guess I've got a convertible now." Sounds just like New England to me.

What is the soul of New England? Something inward, something a little cold even, at least that's how it's going to strike a newcomer. But something fiercely determined, and even more fiercely protective. Almost relishing discomfort. Able to endure almost any adversity, and just get stronger. The one thing that may sicken it is too much ease and prosperity — which, indeed, I suspect is true for almost every region with a soul. Somewhat more tied to the past than any other part of America except a little bit of the South. It has a longer past *to* be tied to than any other part of America except a little bit of the South.

And yet any living soul can change, and must. New ideas

gather in New England with some frequency. Once it was the idea that slavery should be abolished. Then the idea that everybody should be educated. Right now two ideas are strong. And hence two changes I have seen in my own conservative Vermont over the past twenty years are first a mighty tide of environmentalism and second a very rapid alteration in the relation between the sexes.

One of the events I missed during my week at Riverside was a barn-raising on a new organic farm on the other side of town. When I got back, an aged neighbor (still able to use a hammer) was telling me about it. He had been there, helping. "You ain't going to believe this," he said gleefully. "They was twenty carpenters up on that roof — and damn near half of them was *wimmen!*"

There are barn-raisings still to come in New England. New Englanders of every stripe will be up there, hammering and talking, preserving the sense of community that has kept us going for the past three hundred years.

[1989]

# The Body of New England

∾

NEW ENGLAND IS A REMARKABLY small place. The whole region, from the southern border of Connecticut to the north-
ernmost tip of Maine, would fit comfortably inside any one of half
a dozen Midwestern states. There are *counties* in the Far West
bigger than . . . well, yes, bigger than Rhode Island, of course,
but everyone knows that Rhode Island is small. There are also
western counties — around fifty of them — bigger than Connecticut. There is one county in California in which you could gently
put down Vermont and New Hampshire side by side, and still
have room left over for Boston and its suburbs.

And yet, despite its miniature size, New England has had a
lasting impact. For a couple of hundred years it dominated — it
almost was — American culture. It still has influence out of proportion to its square mileage. It still has an unmistakable per-
sonality, a kind of cool private reserve that people from other and
more enthusiastic parts of the United States often find infuriating.
Under the cool exterior, of course, is a good deal of hot pride.

I'm going to be un–New England. I'm going to boast openly,
just as if I were a Texan talking ranch sizes or a Californian on the
dimensions of fruit. Here is what I claim:

New England has more historic buildings, more art masterpieces, more fine old campuses, more beautiful gardens, more
good music, more farms that you might want to stop and take a
picture of — in short, more esthetic pleasure to give — than any

other region of the United States. In the oldest part of New England, all this is present in more concentrated form than anywhere else in the world, except possibly Holland and Belgium.

Take something particularly easy to document. Take the distribution of art museums across the United States. Texas is thirty-two times the size of Massachusetts, and it has about triple the population. But if you look in Lila Sherman's authoritative *Art Museums in America*, you find that little Massachusetts has thirty-six museums worth listing. Giant Texas — Houston, Dallas, and all — has twenty-four.

There are cities, and not particularly big ones, in New England that in terms of art rank equal to half a western state. I'm thinking particularly of Worcester and of Springfield.

Worcester is a city of 160,000, about forty-five miles west of Boston. Anywhere but Massachusetts, it would be counted one of the great art centers of its region. There's the Worcester Art Museum, of course, with its Rembrandts and Raphaels and Rubenses. But that hardly exhausts the city's resources. The American Antiquarian Society is also to be found in Worcester — and it is *the* center for early American documents. But the society has not forgotten art. It also owns (and exhibits) about 150 early American paintings, many of them by our greatest masters, such as John Singleton Copley. And then there's the Higgins Armory of Worcester. Besides one of the world's great collections of arms and armor (all small boys adore the place), the Higgins has paintings. One by Brueghel, for example.

As for Springfield, a slightly smaller city right in the middle of Massachusetts, it has four museums clustered around one central green. I won't make any embarrassing comparisons with Tucson.

But New England's strength in art is even greater than that. The very colleges have collections that might be the envy of a small nation. Take Yale. There exists there something called the Yale Center for British Art. It contains 1,200 paintings by people like Gainsborough and Turner, and 10,000 drawings. Not bad for dinky little New Haven, Connecticut. But if you go look, don't think you've seen the main collection in town. *That* you will find in the Yale University Art Gallery, which is very grand indeed, though not quite so grand as the cluster of art museums at Harvard.

Then there's the more modest (but still princely) collection owned by Dartmouth College in New Hampshire. When was that first opened to the public? 1793. There are even New England prep schools with major art open to the public. I'm thinking especially of the Addison Gallery of American Art at Phillips Andover Academy, thirty miles from Boston. It has "the very finest paintings" of Winslow Homer and Thomas Eakins, says one authority.

But no traveler likes to spend every minute of free time indoors, even looking at Winslow Homers and Brueghels. So, out to the garden. This country is full of beautiful gardens, many of them open to the public. Guess which part is fullest. I'm quoting now a new book called *The Traveler's Guide to American Gardens*. This work is copyrighted by the Garden Club of Georgia. You might expect such a book to give a little special emphasis to southern gardens. After all, gardens really do thrive in warm climates. Sure enough, the *Guide* lists forty-four gardens worth seeing in the state of Georgia, and no less than fifty in Florida. Also two in Nevada.

But the authors, with fine impartiality, assess every garden everywhere in terms of its beauty and its historic importance. They play no regional favorites. The result is that they list fifty-seven in little Massachusetts, thirty-four in still smaller Connecticut, and twenty-three in tiny Rhode Island. If you're a garden lover, you start with New England.

You don't necessarily start in New England for music, though once you would have. You would have in 1714, for example, when the first pipe organ in the Colonies arrived in Boston. Or in 1810, when Gottlieb Graupner, the former oboist in Franz Joseph Haydn's London orchestra, started the Philo-Harmonic Orches-

tra in Boston. (It was small, to be sure: only fifteen players.) Or in
1823, when the quite separate Handel and Haydn Society of
Boston wrote to Beethoven to commission an oratorio. Beethoven
was interested, too, though he didn't get around to composing it
in the four years of life he had left. Or almost any time between
1925 and 1950, a period when it seemed self-evident to most
critics that the Boston Symphony Orchestra was the best in the
country.

But even now, when there are at least a dozen great orchestras
spread across the United States, and only one of them in New
England, even now the region does all right. Not as well as a place
like Bloomington, Indiana, but all right. Every little way you will
find a chamber orchestra, a resident string quartet, a music festival. I think, for example, of the Apple Hill Chamber Players of
Keene, New Hampshire, and of the Marlboro Music Festival in
southern Vermont, presided over for so many years by Rudolf
Serkin. (Who was once given a farm tractor on the stage — like
many adoptive New Englanders, Serkin had a taste for rusticity.)

At this minute, as I write, my little rural state of Vermont is
wracked by a bitter quarrel. Over what? A change in dairy policy? Well, we *are* having a fight over that. Some farmers and
nearly all the ag researchers at the University of Vermont want to
see cows getting shots of bovine somatotrophin to increase their
milk production, sort of the way athletes take steroids. Let's hope
the cows don't later get cancer, the way the athletes are.

But we're having a still bigger fight over whether the trustees
did right to fire the conductor of the Vermont Symphony Orchestra. I don't say every person in the state is stewing over it; I do say
the percentage is higher than it would be of New Yorkers outraged over the Philharmonic. For one thing, the Philharmonic has
never played in every town in New York State.

That's one side of New England: the dense concentration of
culture — and not just painting, music, and gardens, but almost
anything you'd care to name. Literature? If you look at the list of

great American writers, somewhere around half are from New England, somewhere around half from the rest of the country. Sculpture? Let's put it this way. The National Park Service operates about fifty National Historic Sites. Mostly these are political sites — birthplaces of U.S. presidents, etc. — though there are also a few old forts. And then there is exactly one that celebrates the visual arts. Where may that be? In Cornish, New Hampshire. There you'll find the St. Gaudens National Historic Site: a beautiful house and grounds, loaded with statuary by America's greatest sculptor. Nowhere else in the country do park rangers guard this sort of thing, let alone arrange for Sunday afternoon concerts in what was once Augustus St. Gaudens's studio.

The other side of New England is quite different. This is the New England of farms and second-home developments and lobstermen, of big old wooden summer hotels and of stone walls enfolding hill pastures. Of mountain slopes covered with tamarack trees and valleys full of ski chalets. And of just about a thousand beautiful villages.

This New England is to be found mostly, though not entirely, in the periphery. Think of New England as having two parts. The core, the original core of the region, consists of the eastern half of Connecticut, the eastern half of Massachusetts, all of Rhode Island, and a little strip of New Hampshire along the coast. This is where the Pilgrim fathers did their pilgriming, and where the concept of New England (and possibly of the United States) began, 350 years ago.

In 1643 there were six British colonies in the North — that is, north of the Dutch in what is now New York and the Swedes in what is now New Jersey. All were tiny. One midget colony was called Plymouth and one was called Massachusetts-Bay; both were in the eastern part of what is now the state of Massachusetts. Down in Connecticut were two more puny settlements: one called Connecticut and one called the Jurisdiction of New Haven. All were afraid of being wiped out at any minute — by the

French, by the Indians, by the French and Indians acting together.

Representatives from these four met in 1643. They formed
themselves into the United Colonies of New England. Though
the colonies were of different sizes, each was allotted two commissioners. (Later we would call such people senators, and allot two
to each state.) The commissioners had the power to call out the
full military strength of the United Colonies. That is, 100 men
from Massachusetts-Bay and 45 men from each of the other three,
for a total armed force of 235. There was the United States in
miniature.

This core region is what still has most of the high culture and
most of the important cities.

Surrounding the core is a much larger area: all of Maine, all of
Vermont, nearly all of New Hampshire, the western halves of
Connecticut and Massachusetts. All this remains mostly rural.

Not that there isn't culture. For example, if you go about as far
west as you can get in Massachusetts, you come to Williamstown.
Here there is a rather recent college (by eastern Massachusetts
standards) called Williams. Didn't get going until 1793. It has its
own distinguished art museum — and then, about half a mile
from the college, there is another and bigger museum, the Clark.
Some people say it's worth half a day's drive to see the Clark.
Westerners are particularly apt to say that, because one of the
Clark's strengths is its collection of cowboy paintings, especially
Remingtons. But though there are many treats like this in the
periphery, the dominant note is rusticity. Now there are fiddlers'
contests along with the violin concertos.

Two things make rural New England different from most other
rural parts of the United States. One is the unusually high proportion of beautiful old buildings. I'm not claiming there's some
special kind of New England virtue involved — or better taste,
either. There has simply been more time. Take, for example, the
year 1833, a moment when there were no buildings at all in most

of what is now the United States. That year a young Connecticut artist named Charles Eldridge took the stagecoach up to Vermont. His destination was Montpelier, the state capital. It disappointed him. Not enough "size and elegance," he felt. (Montpelier is a junior-size city to this day. Still under 10,000.)

But then he stopped to reflect *why* Montpelier had disappointed him. It was because it had failed to be a climax. For a good reason. "There had been in our route, many villages too beautiful to have a superior even in the principal town." Vermont still has most of those villages, and there are comparable ones throughout the New England periphery. Here are the tall white churches and old clapboard houses that appear on calendars and in the poetry of Robert Frost. They are still beautiful.

The other thing that makes rural New England distinctive is its almost mile-to-mile variability. New England, as I've noted, is quite small by American standards. The miniature quality applies to the scenery as well as the political divisions. Here are not just small states (except Maine) and small counties; here also are low mountains and tiny hidden valleys. Little rivers, but a lot of them. Lakes, but none you'd call great.

There is no grandeur in New England, or almost none. If you want grandeur, you had better head west to the long sweep of a Nebraska prairie, or the three-hundred-mile view from any of many western peaks, or the immense shore of a Great Lake. We have nothing like that in New England. What we do have are hundreds of tiny regions, each with its own slightly different climate, its own special scenery, and often enough its own local stamp on the barns and bridges and house-shutters. In half a day's drive you can reach almost any of them.

[1989]

# V

# Country Battles

# Old MacDonald Lost His Farm

**ꙮ**

ONE OF THE POP HITS OF THE year 1706 was a song that began, "In the fields of frost and snow . . ." It was a farm song, as befitted the rural country England then was. It celebrated the noisy life of an English barn in the winter. In that snug barn, free from the snow, the ducks were quacking, the sheep baaing, the cows mooing, and so on. Those who sang the song imitated every sound.

Pop hits come and pop hits go, but this one stayed on, first for decades and then for centuries. It soon jumped the Atlantic, and over here it evolved into the form every American child knows: "Old MacDonald Had a Farm." In the refrain, the ducks are still quacking, the sheep baaing, the cows mooing.

But though the song is alive and healthy after almost three hundred years, the kind of farm it celebrates is not. There is a terrible silence in the country now, broken only by the occasional rumble of machinery.

Old MacDonald is gone, and so are his animals. Mixed farms, family farms, farms with horses, cows, chickens, pigs, and ducks are vanishing. They remained a normal part of American life until after World War Two. Then, between 1950 and 1990, three million farms were sold or went under — well over half of all the farms we had. We're losing more fast, right now.

That doesn't, of course, mean that the United States is in any danger of running out of food. On the contrary, we have a glut.

The surviving farms are mostly very specialized and very mechanized. At some cost in damage to the ecosystem and at a very high cost in nonrenewable energy — a high-tech American farm consumes around five calories of energy to produce one calorie of food — they turn out gigantic crops.

But it does mean the loss of one of the best ways of life Americans ever had, one Thomas Jefferson thought most of us would always have. A life of hard work, yes, but also of notable independence.

For much of our history, the average American farm was like a miniature kingdom. It produced almost everything its inhabitants needed. That meant that the average farm-dweller, man or woman, possessed several hundred different skills, could turn a hand to almost any job. Could milk cows, deliver baby lambs, herd ducks.

But their skills went far beyond animal care. For example, in my own state of Vermont nobody needed the mid-nineteenth century equivalent of Calvin Klein or Ralph Lauren. Nobody in the country, anyway. They did their own clothes designing, having previously made their own fabrics, tanned their own leather, whittled their own buttons. Here's how an old man named Walter Needham, speaking forty years ago, and quoted in Barrows Mussey's *A Book of Country Things*, described the new-clothes scene in Vermont when his grandfather was a boy:

> Sheep in the old days was one of the most important things a family had. Every farmer had about thirty sheep, which kept him in light, clothes, mutton, and partly in soap. . . . The wool was the principal thing; that was how Gramp got his clothes when he was a boy. If he needed a new pair of pants, they had to shear a sheep; his mother carded the wool, and spun it on a wool wheel. . . . I don't think his mother wove the cloth; that was done on a neighbor's loom, and then she made up the clothes afterward.

Lots of baaing at old MacNeedham's, and lots of creative work.

Self-sufficiency on this scale ended long before 1950. But much remained even after farmers began to buy their wool pants at the store and to get their light from electric bulbs instead of sheep-tallow candles. Even now, the surviving small farmers routinely do fifty or a hundred kinds of work, most of it interesting.

I have a set of neighbors who routinely produce their own table sugar, for example. They know perfectly well that you can go to any grocery store and get five pounds of cane sugar for $1.75. It just suits them to use the considerable skill it takes to make granulated sugar out of maple syrup, and so produce all their own sweetening on their own place, tapping their own trees. They seem to derive the same pleasure from this that someone else might from "getting away" to a hotel in Cancun. I know for sure that I get that same pleasure from making my own butter (from whole milk that I buy, admittedly — I don't keep a dairy cow) and from producing my own heating fuel.

There are many desirable byproducts to such a way of life. One, of course, is that you automatically stay in good shape. The rural village where I live is near enough to a college town so that we get a certain number of joggers jogging through. A man named Bob Stone with whom I sometimes sugar regards them with a mixture of exasperation and amusement. All that strenuous effort, and no product to show for it except something intangible called "feeling good."

"You know what they're doing?" Bob said to me one day, when a pair of joggers went flapping past while we were loading hay. "They're taking their bodies out for a walk, just like you would a dog."

Another consequence of old-fashioned farming — you wouldn't call this one a byproduct — is extra-healthy food. The mechanized farms that now supply ninety-nine percent of what you find in supermarkets certainly produce dependable wheat and milk and corn. There are chemical residues only occasionally.

141

Their chickens, on the other hand, are at least slightly tainted all the time. American chickens live in true ghettos: 100,000 hens jammed together in what is usually called a battery house. They rarely see sunlight. They usually get doctored feed and chemical additives. A free-range hen from a small farm is safer and tastier. And, of course, more expensive in the rare stores where you can find one.

But the most important byproduct of old-fashioned farming is happiness. The pursuit of happiness is something the signers of the Declaration of Independence thought all people were entitled to. I think so, too. Only, it is much easier to pursue in some places than in others. One of the best places to pursue it is when you are living a life pretty much under your own control, in harmony with nature, producing tangible things like food and firewood and woolly sheepskins, doing many kinds of interesting work. The noisy life of Old MacDonald's farm was a kind of rural ode to joy. I find it tragic that such a life should be destroyed to serve no higher end than the profit of agribusiness.

[1987]

# Why I Still (Blush) Heat
with Wood

ᦔ

THE PERCENTAGE OF AMERICAN HOUSEHOLDS that heat with
wood has dropped about fifty percent in the last few years. I've
come to believe that's a good thing. We need to use more oil in this
country. Sort of the way an alcoholic needs to get drunk more
often. Until real trouble comes, the alcoholic isn't likely to think
about reforming. Nor is this country.

What we need is a new oil crisis. Not counting a spill that didn't
really affect many people outside of Alaska, we haven't had one
since 1973. And with oil so plentiful, none seems to be on the
horizon.

So, my reasoning goes, what does the good environmentalist
do? He uses more oil. He certainly doesn't deliberately waste it —
or energy of any kind. But he does substitute fossil fuel for
renewable energy when he conveniently can, and thus contribute
his mite toward bringing on the necessary crisis.

But here's the problem. I just can't make myself do it. It's not
that I'd have to spend any extra money (for me always a painful
prospect). Heating oil is cheap enough at present so that it
wouldn't cost me one extra nickel to switch back. Oh, I might lose
a few hundred dollars in actual cash, since I'd have to buy the oil,
whereas the wood I cut myself. But that thought is deceptive. I
waste a lot of hours in the woods to save those few hundred

dollars. I'm pretty sure that if I just ordered oil, and saved the time for career moves, I would come out ahead financially.

So why, in violation of my conscience and my pocketbook, do I go on heating with wood? Well, there are four reasons.

The first is that I can't seem to get the same kind of comfort out of my oil furnace that I do out of the two woodstoves. The furnace is part of a forced-hot-air system. There are lots of ducts down cellar, and little grates in the floor of each room. It certainly can be very pleasant to come in the house after being out on a cold day, and stand right on one of those grates while hot air blows up your trouser legs.

But it is pleasanter still to stand a couple of feet away from the big woodstove in the living room, and let that radiant heat pour into me. There is no radiant heat from an oil furnace.

Furthermore, I like it that there are several heating zones as you move progressively farther away from a woodstove. Depending on what you're wearing and on your mood, etc., you can read or play checkers or watch TV nearer or farther away. But an oil furnace keeps the whole house at pretty much the same temperature. (Except, in our house, for one room that is at the end of extra-long ducts, and that is always cold.)

Still further, I am one of those people whose nasal passages get all dry in the winter, and who is always pulling out little bottles of saline solution and giving his nose a good spray.

Wood heat doesn't dry the house out nearly as much as oil. I assume that's partly because there's no hot wind blowing whenever I have the stoves going. I know for sure it's partly because I keep a big old iron teakettle simmering on each stove. (And often use the hot water in one of them to shave with, when I don't feel like running the hot water tap in the upstairs bathroom for close to a minute just to get one basin of hot water for shaving.

Finally, I get the comfort of silence. I am one of those people who can be driven almost insane by a persistent dog bark, especially if it's the high-pitched yap-yapping of a terrier. The oil furnace doesn't drive me anywhere near insane — but I can't say I *like* the whistly-whooshy-sighy noise the hot air makes as it gets forced through the ducts. The stoves make about a tenth as much noise. The principal one they do make (unless we're fool enough to burn hemlock and hence get a lot of crackles and mini-explosions) is the really rather cozy sound of an almost-burnt log settling onto the coals. That sound my wife and I both love.

That's the first reason I can't make myself give up the wood-stoves: the heat is so agreeable. The second has to do with staying busy and happy. One of the reasons that I live in the country in the first place is that I like to be physically active. Indeed, I almost need to be. And I much prefer it if the activity seems to be a useful one (as jogging, for example, doesn't).

With a good-sized piece of land to care for and fields to mow, I have no trouble keeping busy all spring, summer, and fall. But then there's winter. In central Vermont, where I live, winter is an extensive period. The ground is frozen for at least four months, and sometimes longer. What can you do then? You can't work the soil, or get stones out of the ground to build walls with, or drive fence posts, or dig ditches.

What you can do is cut trees. Of course I also cross-country ski a little, and have even occasionally gone out on a snow machine. But no way would those two activities last me through the winter, not even if I added snow-shoeing. Instead I am busy and happy out in my woodlot, with my sixteen-inch Jonsered and my twenty-inch Husqvarna. (If you're a fallible chainsaw operator like me, you do well to have two saws with you at all times, so that when you get the first one bound up because you guessed wrong about which way a limb was tensed, you can use the other one to free it.) The Jonsered even has a heated handle — the exhaust can be set to run through it — so that I can saw at zero without my hands hurting.

But you can't be out a whole lot in the winter, because the days are so short. I get fidgety during the long dark evenings, too. And there, too, the stoves help me. I have come to fancy myself rather an expert at raking coals, adjusting logs, all of that. Tending a stove twice during an evening — once in mid-evening and once just before bed — doesn't in fact occupy more than five minutes, but it turns out to be enough to keep the fidgets away. Indeed, I get so addicted to fire-tending that I have distinct withdrawal symptoms at the end of the season. The last short fires are apt to be in late May. By then evenings are very long, and the frozen ground is hardly a memory. But still, for a week or two after the last fire I find myself reaching for the stove shovel, or automatically starting to put the less dangerous-looking junk mail in the little kitchen woodstove — and then remembering that there won't be a fire again until fall.

My stoves keep me comfortable and busy. My wife, too, since she's as good a fire-tender as I, and a better wood-stacker. (You should see the wooden fort she made for her twelve-year-old son. It incorporates about four cords of wood I cut last fall, to use next winter. It's a perfect square blockhouse, about fourteen feet on a side. It has a doorway, windows, loopholes. Marek loves it.)

They also keep my woods nice-looking, and that's the third reason I find it hard to go back to oil. Back before the Arab oil embargo of 1973, before I shifted to wood heat, I already had a chainsaw and I already cut trees. Only then it was just for the occasional sawlog to take to a mill. The tops I had no use for. Well, I could use a small fraction, because we did have a funny little nineteenth-century woodstove in the kitchen — it had come with the house — and we occasionally built a fire in it. But with the furnace roaring away, and the ducts whistle-whooshing streams of warm air, the kitchen of course soon overheated. We mostly just used that stove in early spring and late fall, when the air was cool but the furnace was off.

So what did I do with the top of a yellow birch or a big red oak? I left it where it was. There was only a very small market for firewood back then, and that was mostly for fireplaces. A surprising number of people who bought fireplace wood wanted white birch, because it looks so pretty. (As indeed it does.) Most of the good hardwood tops I would just cut the upper limbs off of, so you wouldn't see the whole skeleton looming up ten feet in the air, and then I'd leave the tangled mess where it was.

Now, of course, I need every single top to feed stoves. I cut the branches up until they're an inch or sometimes even less in diameter, because you can never have too much smallwood. The brushpiles that I leave in the woods are neat and inconspicuous; and they melt right back into the ground in about five years. Whereas whole tree tops. . . . There are even now some pre-1973 skeletons that haven't melted. I admit that they are mostly moss-covered and getting to be attractive — but you should have seen them the first ten years. Hideous.

The fourth reason is sort of scientific. Like everybody else (who has heard of it), I can't help being afraid of the greenhouse effect. Burning wood just doesn't contribute to it the way burning oil or coal or natural gas does.

You know how the greenhouse effect works. Somebody burns something. The carbon in the wood or oil or used kleenex or whatever combines with oxygen in the air. The resulting carbon dioxide then joins the atmosphere, where it proceeds to act as a kind of insulation. The earth gets warmer. Pretty soon the ice caps start to shrink, the ocean rises, and they're going up and down Fifth Avenue in boats.

Of course my woodstoves put carbon dioxide in the air. They do it just as briskly as any oil furnace. But it's carbon dioxide that would have gone into the air anyway, as those treetops in the woods decayed, or as any tree dies of old age and begins to rot. Whereas the carbon in oil and coal and gas is safely locked away underground, and until we haul it out it never meets any oxygen.

Furthermore, the new trees I plant begin to photosynthesize at once, which means they recapture the carbon dioxide as fast or faster than my stoves produce it. Renewable energy is also a renewable atmosphere cleaner. Once you know that, it's a hard fact to ignore. No matter *how* badly we need an oil crisis.

So what do I do? Do Anne and I selfishly keep burning wood, and not help to bring on the crisis we know the country needs? Or do we sacrifice our pleasure for the public good?

We haven't fully decided. But I know which way we are leaning. We have taken a cue from our cats. There is no question at all which they prefer. They are fire worshippers. To be sure, if we use oil, they will each lie on a hot-air vent and be reasonably content. But what pleases them right to the center of their cat-souls is to get as close as they can to a woodstove without actually singeing their fur, and then to shut their eyes and bask. They do not give one thought to needed crises or to the public good. They think hot fur.

I guess we'll think moist nasal passages and clean woods. Let someone else bring on the oil crisis. Maybe the people who buy high-powered speedboats, or pilots in the Air National Guard, who can use up in an hour or two what it would take us all winter to get through. We may be self-centered. But we will stay cozy.

[1990]

# Raining Limes and Lemons

ᢙ

ENVIRONMENTALISTS TEND TO BE lovable people, but it has to be admitted that they exaggerate. A lot. Chicken Little, that excitable hen who raced about informing her neighbors that the sky was about to fall, was the very type of an environmentalist. Ten or fifteen years ago we were all hearing that Lake Erie was "dead." Killed by pollution. "Lake Erie is a cesspool, and it's beyond hope," someone wrote in *Harper's*. But the cesspool got cleaned; and the beaches have reopened, and the blue pike are thriving. Cleveland built a new fishing pier recently. Cleveland is on Lake Erie.

Not only do environmentalists exaggerate, they tend to get mystical. One of their commonest rallying cries is genetic diversity. No species is an island, they say, improving on John Donne; and if some obscure fish — say, the snail-darter — should be obliterated by human beings, why, the very web of life is threatened. They conveniently ignore the fact that species have been going steadily extinct as far back as there is a fossil record, and yet the web of life is seamless still. Human beings had nothing to do with the loss of all those dinosaurs, and probably nothing to do with the extinction of saber-tooth tigers, either. It is simply the case that life-forms are transient. It will be a little sad if the snail-darter goes, but the sky will not fall. Wrong again, Chicken Little.

The problem this makes is that when an environmental crisis really does arrive, too many people are skeptical. Take acid rain.

No one denies that it exists. There are even a few newspapers, like the Charlotte, North Carolina, *Observer*, that routinely include the pH of rainfall in weather reports, just like temperature and humidity.

No one even denies that it has harmful effects. The Adirondack lakes that once had trout and now don't are there to be counted. (Two hundred and twelve is the last count I saw.) The dead spruce trees on Vermont mountains are very visible, and scientists at the University of Vermont have all but proved that acid rain was what killed them.

But despite or maybe even because of the frantic squawking of environmentalists, there's a widespread feeling that the problem is both minor and regional. The East is upset; we want our trout and our mystical feelings. The Midwest, which we correctly blame for most of the acidity, yawns and says jobs and steel mills are more important. The Far West reflects that the prevailing winds move eastward — sulfuric acid from Ohio and Indiana will never harm *them* — and shrugs off the whole thing.

That's why a book like Robert and Alexander Boyle's *Acid Rain* is an important event. It's not a great book, nor is it entirely free from exaggeration and mystical feelings. It's not even complete. But it gathers most of what is known globally about acid rain, and with calm certainty makes a case that no reasonable person can ignore. There is more at stake here than trout and spruce trees. The Far West is not immune. (Nowhere is, and in that sense John Donne was quite right.) The world can deal with acid rain at a reasonable cost now. Or at an appallingly high cost later.

One of the useful things the book does is to give the history of acid rain. It is not new. It was first identified in Manchester, England, in 1852. Then as now, a principal cause was the burning of high-sulfur coal. But then it really was a local problem. It messed up only a few English counties, chiefly in the Midlands.

By 1905 it had begun to turn international: Fish in Norway were dying from sulfuric acid created in the blast furnaces of

Germany. (Though it wasn't until 1959 that the first Norwegian scientist made the connection; for a long time people thought that acid rain merely corroded metal, dissolved marble, things like that.)

Sometime in the 1960s, acid rain became a truly global phenomenon. The chief reason, of course, was that industrialism had also become a truly global phenomenon — and instead of a few thousand tons of sulfur dioxide going into the atmosphere here and there, human beings were putting over a hundred million tons in the air each year. All it had to do was encounter water vapor to become sulfuric acid, and come back down as acid rain, acid snow, even acid fog.

There were other, lesser causes, some of which would be quite funny if they weren't so painful. One was the Clean Air Act passed by Congress in 1970. Before it passed, there were two smokestacks in the United States more than five hundred feet tall. Now there are about 180, as various industries meet the requirements for local clean air by getting their pollution well up into the atmosphere and hence spreading it around the world. In the United States, that has meant that states like Florida, Minnesota, and Colorado are getting an ever-increasing share of acid precipitation.

Another thing the book does is to explain exactly what acid rain does, and that's no mean feat. The Norwegians weren't simply being stupid not to realize for so long what was killing their fish. Acid precipitation works in complicated ways. For one thing, it releases aluminum and other metals naturally occurring in the earth's crust; and it's often metallic poisoning rather than sour water per se that kills most of the life forms in some lake or river. For another, it's as deadly over land as over water. It can react in interesting ways on the finish of cars. A 1978 rainstorm in Pennsylvania left several hundred cars splotched and discolored by sulfuric acid from heaven. That rain was a mere 2.3 on the pH scale — low, but hardly a record. Things have not improved since. They are worse. Rain capable of splotching cars is now so routine that General Motors includes a paragraph in all its car manuals, explaining that it's not their fault but nevertheless promising to repair for free any acid rain damage that occurs in the first year.

If 2.3 can be called "mere," what's a *really* acid rain? The current American record, set in West Virginia, is just under 2. West Virginia would have been better off if large planes had flown overhead, spraying lemon juice. Oh, come, surely I exaggerate. I do not. The bottled lemon juice you buy in stores has a pH of 2.1. The pH scale being logarithmic, that tenth of a point makes quite a difference. The pH scale starts at 7, which is neutral — neither acid nor alkaline. Six is faintly acid. Five is ten times more acid, 4 a hundred times more acid, 3 a thousand times more. Guess what 2 is. In short, lemon juice is a lot less sour than the rain that fell on West Virginia.

People who couldn't care less about trout or spruce trees often do care about their cars. They may also care that aluminum in the water supply is distinctly bad for the health. Those with picture windows may even mind slightly that the average visibility in the Ohio River Valley is down from ten miles in 1939 to four miles now, the chief cause being the sulfate particles in the air.

But is it really fair to blame all that on industry? Pretty much, yes. Another thing the Boyles' book does is to investigate some of the reassuring counter-claims put out by companies that produce sulfur-dioxide pollution. The most dramatic of these is the widely repeated story that acid rain is not some creature of the industrial revolution at all, but an age-old natural phenomenon. The evidence: the acidity of 350-year-old ice cores taken from the Antarctic and the Himalayas.

The Boyles found that story had its genesis in a scientific publication called the *Wall Street Journal*, which ran an article quoting the two researchers at the University of New Hampshire who actually studied the ice cores. They then talked to the two scientists. "The story was extremely distorted," said Dr. Paul Mayewski. "There were no significant heavy-acid traces at all in the cores." Meanwhile, the story had appeared as sober fact in a book called *What We Know About Acid Rain*, put out by the electrical industry. It even popped up in the *Congressional Research Service Review*.

But the most useful thing the book does is to show how easy it would be to get some of that acid out of the air. If Ohio, which all by itself puts about three million tons of sulfur dioxide into the world's air each year from coal burning alone, merely washed the coal before burning it, it would reduce the pollution by somewhere between 500,000 and 700,000 tons. That's not the Boyles' claim; they are just reporting what the state of Ohio's own Advisory Task Force on Acid Rain said. The Task Force wasn't saying a word at this point about scrubbers or any other expensive technology. Just washing the coal.

Of course if you do go on to scrubbers, there is far more that can be done. The greatest single source of acid rain in the entire New World is one enormous smokestack in Canada, owned by the International Nickel Company. In the bad old days (that is, up to about ten years ago) it put nearly two million tons of sulfur dioxide into the air — at a height of nearly a quarter of a mile, for better dissemination all over North America. Pushed hard by the Canadian government, International Nickel began to scrub, and now it scrubs in dear earnest. And the stack emits only a bit over half a million tons annually — still enough to sour a lot of rain, but a mighty improvement.

Pleased with itself for bringing that about, and resenting what Ohio, Illinois, and Indiana generously send north, the Canadian government keeps proposing to the United States government that the two countries bind themselves to reduce their total sulfur dioxide emissions by fifty percent. It's a little bit analogous to the proposals the Russians keep making for joint reduction of weapons. But even though there are no wily perestroikists behind the acid rain idea, only mild bureaucrats, the United States keeps turning the proposal down. Presumably we want to stay Number One in pollution, too.

Finally, the Boyles make some predictions — or at least they quote some made by other people. Here they may be exaggerating. They quote Professor Bernhard Ulrich of Göttingen University as saying that it is already too late to save much of the woodland in Germany. "The first large forests will die in the next five years. They can no longer be saved."

They quote Professor Torbjorn Westermark, a Swedish nuclear chemist, on the possibility that one of the metals released by acid rain, as its pH continues to drop, will be uranium, with a consequent worldwide increase in leukemia. They quote a scenario composed by Professor Herbert Bormann of Yale, in which the final stage is the collapse of whole regional ecosystems, as the lemon juice keeps falling.

Who knows? The three professors may be three Chicken Littles. I sure hope so. What is definite, and what this book documents, is that right now more and more lakes are losing not just their fish but two or three hundred life forms as the merely diluted lemon juice of present rain keeps falling. Seen any frogs lately? More and more aluminum is being released into groundwater. More and more trees are dying, including many maples in Vermont. And the final irony is in one other figure the Boyles quote.

It wouldn't even cost much to reverse the trend. If the National Commission on Air Quality is to be believed, a two percent surcharge on utility bills in the eastern United States would yield enough pollution-control money to reduce the sulfur dioxide in eastern air by fifty percent.

I don't think you have to be a mystic to find that a good idea.

[1984]

# Death of a Farmer

∾

THERE WAS A WEEK IN 1985 when three Iowa farmers killed themselves. None of them knew each other. These were separate tragedies, related only by the fact that all three were responding to the (partly government-generated) crisis in American agriculture. Two of the three were ruined men, about to lose their farms. The third man was in good shape financially. But he was a country banker as well as a farmer. He "committed suicide rather than foreclose on friends."

This is the stuff of melodrama — and in fact it has been the stock form of American melodrama. The villain twirls his mustache and threatens to foreclose on the farm. The farmer's beautiful daughter kneels before him and begs him to spare her father, and the land, and the animals. In the old melodrama she often succeeded. In real America she has not. Four million farms have died so far in this century, two-thirds of all there were. More continue to die now.

Two new books look at American agriculture in exactly complementary ways. They are like the masks of comedy and tragedy that you sometimes see on theater programs: just alike, except that one is smiling and one is downcast.

In *Farm: A Year in the Life of an American Farmer*, Richard Rhodes, the distinguished journalist who grew up in Missouri (and now lives in Cambridge, Massachusetts) has done the smile mask. He spent a year on a successful Missouri farm with a truly happy family named Bauer. Tom Bauer, the father, is forty-six years old, six foot three, 240 pounds. All muscle. He farms 337 acres that he owns, sharecrops on 779 more. Like most successful farmers, he understands high technology. He can figure out the wiring in a damaged combine without even a manual. Besides his own combine, he owns four trucks, four tractors, a Kawasaki three-wheeler for getting out to the barn, an air hammer, complete welding equipment, a 7,200-bushel metal grain bin.

All of this he can and does fix himself. His college-age son Wayne, who has eye problems but wants to be a farmer anyway, can fix most of it, too. His daughter Sammi, who is nine, can drive the Kawasaki — and in a real pinch, when they're harvesting the corn and soybeans, a pickup truck, too. His wife Sally can and often does handle the giant combine, a job that calls for great skill.

Tom Bauer also knows how to deal with the government, and with banks, and with his fertilizer man, his feed man, his propane man. He has several hundred different skills, and he uses them all.

About this family Richard Rhodes has written a wonderful book. He means Tom to stand for American agriculture in general, as can be seen by the names he chose. Because these are such intimate portraits, Rhodes adopted pseudonyms for both people and places. Tom, like many Missouri farmers, is of German descent. Rhodes calls him Tom Bauer. Bauer means "farmer" in German; we have Tom Farmer. And where does T. F. live? In Crevecoeur County, Missouri. *That* Rhodes named after St. John de Crèvecoeur, who in 1782 published the first American best-seller. It's called "Letters From an American Farmer." De Crèvecoeur said that the best person in the world was an American farmer. Reading Rhodes, you can easily believe it.

Bruce Brown has a much sadder story to tell in *Lone Tree*. His farmer was another big man, an Iowan named Dale Burr. In 1985 he was about to see his farm foreclosed on by a somewhat grasping banker in Iowa City. Dale's son John seemed about to lose his, too. Something snapped in Dale, who one December morning killed his wife, the banker, and then in a death of heroic agony (he misjudged the angle of the shotgun and, horribly wounded, had to manage to reach the trigger again) he killed himself.

If Tom Bauer stands for the farmers who succeed, then Dale Burr stands for the larger number who are failing. So he must be less at ease with high technology, not so good at fixing combines, more awkward with bankers, right? Wrong. Dale Burr was an exceptionally good farmer, and exceptionally at home in banks. (His father, like many rich farmers sixty years ago, had essentially controlled a small one.)

Several things combined to destroy Dale Burr. But the central one was precisely that he was such a high-tech, high-finance, almost agri-biz kind of guy. As the government teaches and tells farmers to do, he and his son both expanded on credit — borrowing money to buy more land, higher-tech equipment, fancier hybrid seed. For a time it worked. Then a cycle of land prices ended. Iowa farm values dropped abruptly, and both men found themselves owing banks more than they were worth. Farm values dropped in Missouri, too — but Tom Bauer was old-fashioned. He would never borrow more than $25,000 at a time, and so survived. There is a moral here.

I exaggerated a little when I said these two books are identical, except that one is happy and one is sad. Rhodes's is much better written. He is a master storyteller, and he brings the Bauers and their farm fully to life. Bruce Brown is a good and careful journalist, but he has no such skill as that. Furthermore, he occasionally does what I think is called "dumping the files" — including some detail, such as how Dale Burr liked the Iowa State Fair when he was ten years old, chiefly because the information was available.

There is another difference, too, this one in Brown's favor. He is much better at putting present farming in the context of American history. Our government has always been working for or against the family farm (usually against — George Washington and Alexander Hamilton were hot at it two hundred years ago), and Brown has fascinating details to give. Rhodes devotes one piece of a chapter to this larger picture, but the reader gets no such overview as in Brown.

But the two books *are* alike, even down to both being slightly dated in the same way. Neither betrays by a flicker that the kind of high-tech, high-debt, high-fertilizer, high-herbicide farming that is now standard in America may be about to come to an end. Rhodes does repeat that wonderful joke: "A farmer is someone who launders government money for a chemical company." And he does mention that Tom Bauer would prefer to farm without pesticides, if he believed that were possible. But nowhere in either book is there the faintest hint that low-input farming and organic farming may be the wave of the future. There is already organic iceberg (ugh) lettuce being grown by at least one agribiz corporation.

Partly because it is free of these blinkers, Mark Kramer's *Three Farms* remains the landmark book on American farming. (It contains the best account of big California farms I have ever seen.) But Rhodes has written a book worthy to sit on the shelf near Kramer, and Brown has brought together a mass of riveting information. The one is a joy to read, and the other will richly repay study.

[1989]

# The Price Is Wrong

∿

LAST FALL MY WIFE AND I had our two pigs butchered. They were belted Hampshires: pretty things (as pigs go), big and frisky, organically raised with plenty of room *to* frisk.

We did none of the work ourselves. We didn't even deliver the pigs. The slaughterer drove five miles out from town and picked them up in his truck. I was not there to help.

Back in town, he slaughtered them, scalded the carcasses, scraped off the bristles, dressed them out, and finally sawed each pig in half lengthways. Then he delivered the four sides to the meatcutter. A few days later the cutter called to tell us our pigs were ready. My wife swung by on her way home from work, and he loaded two huge boxes of meat into the back of her Blazer.

You know those supermarket games where you can have as much free food as you can pull off the shelves in ninety seconds? No frantically filled cart ever bulged with even nearly as big a load as either of those boxes. There were pork chops in neatly wrapped packages. Crown roasts, spareribs, lard. This skilled country butcher had ground and made up our sausage — lots of sausage, in one-pound packages. We got everything back but the hams and bacon, which were still out being smoked.

What did we pay for all that? Well, let me counter with another question. What do you think a fair price would have been? Remember, we were getting a year's worth of pork for our whole

159

family. Plus a little extra to swap with my wife's sister and her family, who raise sheep on the other side of town.

True, we furnished the pigs. But the price includes loading them — and pigs are hard animals to load — trucking them, four separate operations by the slaughterer, about a dozen by the butcher. He even provided spices for the sausage.

You're ready? OK, the answer is $52 for the slaughterer, $84.14 for the butcher.

Just to put that in context, let me mention some other things you could get around here for the same money. "Here" is St. Johnsbury, Vermont. For $84.14 you could get a lawyer to sit comfortably in his office chair and talk to you for an hour. (If some lawyer is thinking scornfully I must be pretty ignorant about legal fees — *he* doesn't know anybody who charges $84.14 an hour — let me say I don't either. But I know plenty who charge $75 and plenty more who charge $100. I'm just averaging. Incidentally, I also know a psychotherapist in Newton, Massachusetts, who charges $140 for fifty minutes. A full two pigs' worth. And I've heard about a college counselor in New York who charges $400 an hour. A six-pig man.)

Let's start again. For $84.14 you could spend nearly five hours lying in bed in one of our local hospitals, provided you didn't take any medicines or anything; the big hospital in this region has a basic room charge of $410 a day. You could stay almost the whole night at a good country inn.

What about $52? Well, you could stay the whole night at a fairly good motel. You could replace one-sixth of one fender on your car, provided you drive one of the cheaper and easier-to-fix models. You could buy the second-best pair of leather gloves in the Land's End catalogue. You could pay one day's tuition at Dartmouth College.

By now you see what I'm getting at. We live in a country where food and the local processing of food are cheap, compared to practically everything else. No wonder agriculture is in such deep trouble. No wonder farmers are going bankrupt in such large numbers. Milk prices (to the farmer) stay level, or go down. Everything else doubles, then triples. How can the farmer pay the inflated cost of lawyers, hospitals, car repairs with his deflated milk check?

Law schools are crowded at the moment, schools of agriculture nearly empty. (OK, I exaggerate. But they are smaller than they were.) What is the advantage to the country of still more lawyers? Doubtful at best. How many corporate takeovers, hostile *or* friendly, with their attendant swarms of lawyers, have produced any benefit for humanity? And yet of course ambitious young men and women are going to take worthless or even harmful jobs in corporate law as long as the pay is so lavish. Of course the rural world is going to go on collapsing as long as farmers lose money.

The question I really want to raise is *why* so many farmers are losing money. The government's answer for a long time has been that we are seeing a shake-out, as small farmers fail, and then medium-sized farmers fail, and finally the country moves entirely into profitable agribusiness. And that is a true answer, but a very narrow one.

Another answer is that we have a deliberate policy in this country of cheap food. The government's energies for a hundred years and more have been mainly directed toward larger, cheaper crops, and never mind the cost to the ecosystem. Of course the Department of Agriculture has promoted some very good conservation practices over the years, and it still occasionally does. But the general thrust has been quite different. Mine the groundwater, it advises. Drain the Colorado River; the government will help you do it. Slather the earth with pesticides and herbicides. Use up the natural gas to make chemical fertilizer. Do all this to keep food cheap. The deferred costs won't show up in their full dimensions for another generation.

I have to say it's worked. The average American spends only eleven percent of his or her income on food. No one else in the world spends so little, even though Americans eat so much. The French devote seventeen percent of their income to food, the Japanese twenty percent. The Irish lay out twenty-four percent, Mexicans thirty-one percent, Greeks thirty-seven percent, and so on. Even Canadians, our nearest rivals in this matter, have food bills a quarter again as high as ours. What we spend *our* money on is health care — some of it made necessary, of course, by unhealthy food.

Still a third answer is that most farmers only produce food. They don't often process it, and they don't often sell it directly to consumers. It has so worked out in this country that processing and marketing are where the money lies.

To take one local example, we have an ice cream company in Vermont, a company that emphasizes its use of Vermont milk and cream. In fact, the founders pretty much built the company on that concept. So much so that when they recently bought an ice cream plant in Wisconsin, they made the decision to ship Vermont milk and cream out there, rather than leave the magical words "fresh Vermont cream" off the cartons.

This company is one I greatly admire. I think it shows more sense of environmental responsibility than almost any other corporation in the country. I also like the taste of their ice cream. But the fact remains that the founders of that company are millionaires, and the Vermont farmers from whom they buy milk are no richer than before. They are, to be sure, still in business.

What it seems to me is that farmers need more and more to get into processing and retail distribution. It won't be easy. Most laws and regulations are written to make it as hard as possible for a small producer to process food, or to sell it if he does. If my wife and I had raised four pigs, for example, and wanted to sell the meat of two of them, we couldn't have. We could advise people where to go to college, but we couldn't sell pork. Not legally. It's true our pigs are organically raised, brilliantly healthy, free of both the stress and the medication of a big Iowa corn-and-hog operation — but unless they went to a slaughterhouse where a full-time government inspector was on duty, no selling any of their meat. You can imagine how many small country slaughter-houses can afford a full-time government inspector.

Naturally the government's indignant answer would be that they're only thinking about health. I would be more impressed with this answer if I didn't know about the conditions in the plants where broiler chickens are processed. The inspectors are right there, and nevertheless the line of birds being processed moves right along through a sort of soup of chicken feces. There is certainly an idealistic component in some of the laws that keep farmers from processing much of the food they grow; there is also visible the guiding hand of big business.

Many things can be said in favor of cheap food. In America the biggest of them is that it gives people much greater freedom as to how they spend their incomes. In some other parts of the world it is of course a matter of life and death. We are lucky indeed to have the lowest grocery bills on earth.

But the price the whole world is paying for our cheap food almost staggers the mind. The price we ourselves pay is that of rapidly destroying rural America, and somewhat less rapidly using up our natural resources. There is currently an argument as to whether we expend more like four or more like ten calories of energy for every calorie of food we produce. Nearer ten, I think, when you add packaging and transportation to what farmers themselves consume. Either way, it's a rotten equation. American agribusiness runs an energy deficit that makes the government's dollar deficit seem piddling. It can't last.

The price the rest of the world pays along with us is in damage to the planet. They spray DDT in Panama so that Americans can eat cheap beef. They spray worse things than that in Indonesia to keep our spices cheap. Iowa topsoil slides into the Mississippi River at about the rate of two tons per acre per year, principally to keep the price of corn down. The last figure I heard was that the

United States all by itself creates about a quarter of the pollution in the entire world. A huge share of that is in toxic chemicals used in agriculture — somewhere around eighty-seven percent of all pesticides we produce, for example.

The worst part about our world-record low food prices is that they lock American farmers ever more tightly into the present high-input, high-output, high-pollution, high-waste system. There is no room to think about environmental damage if you're constantly struggling to increase your yield per acre or per cow, just in order to survive.

But let's be cheerful. Let's suppose you wanted to unlock the farmers. Could you do it? Sure. There are even several ways.

One would be to copy Switzerland and Canada, and establish a farm quota system. Actually, we already have a rudimentary quota system in the United States — but it is one that *encourages* heavy use of herbicides and other toxics. The Swiss or Canadian way is to agree that a given farm shall produce so many bushels of soybeans or hundredweight of milk. The farmer is assured that there will be a market and a decent price for what he grows. And since there is a ceiling on quantity, the way he can raise his income is to work on quality. Meanwhile, he needn't abuse his land just in order to keep going.

The current American way is for the government to pay farmers to take a certain number of acres out of production. The theory is that they'll produce less on the remaining acreage, and so there won't be another glut of corn or wheat. What actually happens is that the farmer doubles the quantity of chemicals he puts on the remaining acres, crops just as intensely as he knows how — and manages to produce about as much as he would have using gentler methods on the whole farm. The whole system is a sort of guarantee of environmental degradation. But it is a system that has evolved over many years. There are lots of vested interests. The Department of Agriculture is not at all likely to reform the system any time soon — and Congress probably wouldn't let the department if it tried.

Another way would be to extend the pay-to-pollute laws to farming. Put a good hefty tax on all the pesticides and herbicides, and maybe a smaller tax on chemical fertilizers. It wouldn't matter (to me, anyway) whether the chemical company paid the tax at the time of production or the farmer paid it when he bought. Either way, the cost of toxic farming would increase, thus creating a space for healthy farming.

I think it's even less likely that the government will do that, over the outraged cries of Dupont, Monsanto, and Dow.

The real serious hope lies not in anything Congress or the states may do. It lies with individual consumers. Right now there are many millions of Americans who prefer natural foods, even organically grown foods — when they can get them at the same price. There are at least two or three million people in the country who will pay a premium for organic produce. The willingness seems to be greatest in New England and in California. It is that willingness that enables organic farmers to farm in a way that entirely or almost entirely avoids harm to the planet. With the organic premium, the price is right. Organic farmers can be stewards of the earth and still make a profit. They don't have to be exploiters.

Most of us feel a great reluctance to pay the premium, however. I know I do. Even though I raise organic pigs and sometimes organic cows, even though I believe we are in the process of polluting our planet beyond retrieval, I *still* feel a reluctance to pay $1.29 for an organic avocado when I can get the regular pesticide-grown ones in the adjoining bin for only $1.09.

I even mind a little that organically grown oranges don't have a uniformly orange color — that is, I miss whatever chemical dye it is that they spray on "regular" oranges. (The organic ones do seem to taste a little better, though, once you get through the rind.)

My one serious hope is that enough of us will get scared about our health so that we will pay the premium. Eventually spend maybe 14.5 percent of our incomes on food, as Canadians do. Then the best and wisest conventional farmers, the ones who are appalled at what they are doing to their own land, will be able to shift to sustainable methods and still make money. At some point in this transition, the supermarket chains will have to open themselves to organic produce, as they now do not, or risk losing too many customers to alternative stores.

But first I and people like me need to teach ourselves to pay sixty-nine cents instead of fifty-nine cents for winter carrots. Planetarily, the price is right.

[1990]

# The Lesson of the Bolt Weevils

∾

PROBABLY THE SHARPEST QUESTION facing an environmentalist in the 1990s is what to do about the law. Does a good environmentalist stay law-abiding and work within the system? Obviously the traditional answer is yes, of course. That's what democracy means.

But what if the system seems to be corrupt? What if the very people in the system who are charged with protecting the environment are the ones who betray it? What if the Forest Service itself builds roads at taxpayer expense in order to facilitate the clearcutting of great swaths of our national forests? What if high officials of the Environmental Protection Agency simply announce that they've decided not to enforce the laws the environmentalists got passed? *This* deadline for atmospheric clean-up they've unilaterally decided to extend for three years; *that* regulation for strip-mining they've decided to ignore indefinitely.

Does the good environmentalist sigh a little and start gathering signatures for a new petition? Go back to court yet again? Or does he or she turn militant and stage a sit-in in the national forest? Maybe even drive spikes into the great, helpless trees, so that when the loggers come, their chainsaws will chatter to a halt?

It's a hard decision, and one the environmental movement has by no means come to a consensus about. At one extreme are those who say that ecosabotage is criminal behavior, to be treated like any other crime. And not only criminal, but counterproductive — it forfeits public sympathy. Dangerous, too. Hidden spikes may endanger loggers' lives. At least once, they already have.

At the other extreme are those who say that ecosabotage is the only way left, at this eleventh hour, to save our planet. Yes, it's dangerous, but it's also dramatic. So far from forfeiting general sympathy, the ecosaboteur brings it into being. Spiked trees get the public's attention in a way that petitions never have and never will. Court cases have their place — a major one — but what we as a people are really moved by is stories, not lawyers' arguments.

They must be true stories, too; they must really have happened. There are hundreds of novels about nuclear disaster, some of them masterpieces, like *A Canticle for Leibowitz*. There are dozens of movies. None has had even a fraction of the conversionary force that Chernobyl did, or Three Mile Island.

Or think back to abolition days. Abolitionists petitioned and held public meetings for thirty years. What finally roused the nation was a criminal act. John Brown, that abo-saboteur, had to raid the federal arsenal at Harper's Ferry, and be caught, and be put to death before his fellow Yankees moved against slavery in real earnest.

Not only that, some environmentalists insist, ecosabotage often *is* productive. The spikes will often save the actual trees they're driven into. The timber corporation will be disgusted at the costly delays. It will be fearful of all the publicity now attached to its turning a stretch of national forest into a sorry mass of stumps. It will withdraw its crews.

What continues to surprise me is that neither side in this long debate seems to look much at the one major example of ecosabotage we have had so far in the United States. A pity. Because it offers profound lessons for both sides. And, of course, an exciting story, too.

168

That story begins in Minnesota in 1972. The opening scene is quiet enough: we see a small and very private meeting. Officials of two Minnesota power companies (both technically co-ops) have gathered to plan a giant new coal-burning power plant. It's going to be a pretty good polluter. They decide to put it in the middle of North Dakota, next to the strip mine that will feed it.

They will then build a 430-mile power line, cutting across North Dakota and Minnesota to just outside the suburbs of Minneapolis. It will be the largest direct-current line in the United States, carrying 800,000 volts of electricity. It will run on a strip of land 160 feet wide. A strip 160 feet by 430 miles will consume about 9,000 acres of land. Along that strip the companies will erect a long row of steel towers — just under 1,700 of them. Each will be 180 feet high. At the very top the big wires will run.

Almost no one likes to live under high-voltage lines. So how do you persuade them to? The answer, if you're a utility company, is that you don't have to. You can force them to. Utilities are generally able to borrow the government's power of eminent domain. They send the appropriate agencies a projection showing that the power will be needed. After a number of hearings, approval is usually forthcoming.

That doesn't mean there won't be loud outcries from those who wind up under the line. In a democracy, such cries are expected. To counter their effect, the Minnesota companies decide to site the line "objectively." They hire an out-of-state firm to do it by computer. The computer is given a point system to work with — the more points a piece of land is awarded, the less danger of its having a power line across it. Land owned by the state of Minnesota gets five points, woodland is worth three points, and so on. Farmland, however, gets no points at all. Zero. Naturally, the computer plots the line, often diagonally, across one farm after another. Many of the farms will be cut in two.

The farmers, of course, know nothing about these plans — not even that there's going to be *be* a power line. There's a good case for power-company secrecy, too. If word got out, wouldn't speculators be buying up possible right-of-way land, hoping to get a high price? You bet.

Two years go by. The power companies complete their plans. They ask for and get the largest loan ever given by the Rural Electrification Administration. They award the first $150 million in contracts.

Now it's time to start acquiring the right-of-way. At this moment the farmers learn what is about to happen. They are outraged. The way they see it, everything has been kept secret until so much money has been committed that there can be no serious question of not building the line. At most, you might hope to push it over onto someone else's land.

But it so happens that this new plant will produce far more electricity than the customers of the two companies will be able to use for many years. It further happens that both companies have inverted rate structures — the more you use, the less you pay per kilowatt. And both actively promote what many consider to be inefficient uses of electricity, such as electric heating for houses in a cold climate. All this sets some farmers thinking. Maybe the line isn't needed. Maybe if the companies promoted conservation instead, it would never be needed.

Thoughts turn to action. In two of the counties the line is scheduled to cross — Pope and Stearns — the farmers do what farmers seldom do. They organize. They decide to oppose the line — legally, of course. At that time, anything even faintly illegal would have shocked them. Many of these farmers are Norwegian-American, and incredibly law-abiding. Many have never had so much as a traffic ticket.

Very soon, they score a success. In Minnesota at that time, the right to use eminent domain was granted county by county, with state supervision. And in Pope County, the commissioners do something unheard of. They deny it.

But the law is just in the middle of changing. Power is to be centralized in the state Energy Agency. By a quick legal coup the power companies are able to transfer their request, and they shrug off the authority of Pope County. One down.

So the farmers hire a lawyer of their own and go to court. They are going to present two arguments: first, that the line is unnecessary, and second, that it may be dangerous. There are as-yet-unknown hazards in so huge a direct-current voltage. You could safely bury the big wires, of course, as the companies already plan to do when they near Minneapolis — but the whole line? Ridiculous, the companies say. It would cost seventeen times as much.

To the farmers' surprise and indignation, they are not allowed to present their arguments. Neither one is relevant, the judges say. What would be relevant? Well, if some farmer could show just cause why the line should not cross his land and therefore should cross some neighbor's land, that would be relevant. Appealed to, the state supreme court agrees.

By now, the people in Pope and Stearns counties are beginning to distrust the system. If they could have known what the deputy director of the Minnesota Pollution Control Agency would later say (just after resigning), they would have felt even more distrustful. He said he'd come to believe that his agency and the state Environmental Quality Council — both involved with the power line — were "set up to aid large corporations in getting around local government."

In June 1976, when surveyors for the companies began to lay out the line in Stearns County, they were met by a crowd of about sixty farmers blocking their path. The farmers were polite but determined. A little angry, too. Angry, for example, that when they had taken an appeal to the Environmental Quality Council, the hearing was presided over by a brand-new state official — an employee of the council whose previous job had been with the consulting firm in Michigan that sited the power line in the first place. They considered that suspicious.

Some of the farmers had their tractors with them; a few were on horseback. The surveyors retreated.

They were soon back, accompanied by reluctant local law

officers. Over the next few weeks, the blocking party grew to several hundred men and women. There was little violence, just a lot of civil disobedience. Almost all of it occurred on land actually owned by one or another of the demonstrators. Many farmers had trouble believing that it was an indictable offense to demonstrate on their own land. A few people got arrested; a few went to jail.

These demonstrations spread from county to county in western Minnesota, and for a time the surveying almost stopped. Then the companies struck back. They started filing half-million-dollar damage suits against individual farmers. Arrests are one thing, but a suit that could cost you your farm is another. A lot of demonstrators withdrew.

But in Pope County, among other places, the resistance continued, and it began to get rougher. Survey stakes tended to vanish as soon as they were planted. By January 1978, the survey was still incomplete, though more than two hundred state troopers (out of a total state force of five hundred) were now patrolling the power line rather than the roads. That month, the Pope County attorney resigned rather than prosecute a group of newly arrested demonstrators.

Two hundred troopers can patrol a lot of power line, especially if they are helped by three hundred newly hired security guards. By summer, the survey was complete, and the 1,685 steel towers were fast going up. It was then that the Minnesota bolt weevils appeared.

The towers that carry a high-voltage line are somewhat like things you'd build from an erector set, only much, much bigger. They are held together with huge steel bolts. Unbolt the base of one, and at considerable risk to yourself you may be able to bring it down. On the night of August 2, 1978, the first tower crashed. Within a week, three more came plunging down.

No one has ever been convicted of sabotaging those towers, though it's not for lack of trying. The companies offered a reward of $50,000 for information, and later upped the price to $100,000. No takers. Instead the towers continued to crash. Over the next year, ten more came hurtling down, and many others were unsuccessfully assaulted. About midway in that year the companies gave technical ownership of the line to the federal government, so the FBI could come in. (The companies reassumed title in 1985. To the farmers, one more bit of legal sleight of hand.) The FBI caught no bolt weevils, either.

The farmers also didn't stop the line. The full force of the state of Minnesota was too much for them. The line was energized ten years ago, and it has been in use ever since. A couple of more towers toppled as lingering acts of defiance — the final one on the night of August 2, 1983, the fifth anniversary of the first. All has been peaceful since.

So what did all those criminal acts accomplish?

Well, quite a lot. For one thing, the companies had originally intended to build another seventy-eight-mile line, the so-called Wilmarth Extension. It remains unbuilt, and most people in Minnesota agree that violent resistance to the original line is the reason. More important, *any* new power line in Minnesota would now have to be justified in advance far more rigorously than this one was. The man who was governor of Minnesota at the time the towers crashed is on record as saying it is because of the farmers' actions that his state now has what he claims are the best energy-control laws in the nation.

More important still, the ripple effect has reached well beyond Minnesota. Not in public perception, because there hasn't been much of that, but in professional energy circles. It has reached Texas, for example. There, a similar 800,000-volt direct-current line has been killed by the Texas Public Utilities Commission. The Texas commissioners were swayed by a health study, done in Minnesota at the time the last towers were crashing down and undertaken because they were. That study was inconclusive — nowhere near proof enough to persuade Minnesota to take the line down again. But it raised enough doubts, particularly about ionized air, to stop the new one in Texas.

And then there is a final effect that is highly ironic. One of the arguments the Minnesota farmers wanted to make in court was that a high-voltage DC line may have special dangers — may be worse for people and animals living within its magnetic field than the more usual alternating current lines. Silenced in court, they resorted to ecosabotage; and one consequence of their expensive ($6 million in damage), destructive, risky, illegal action was to encourage a more careful study of power lines in general than had hitherto been done in this country. As a very indirect and indeed unprovable effect, research got funded that might not have otherwise.

It now begins to look as if DC lines are actually safer, though as the Texas commissioners point out, this is far from proven. But don't relax: what that means is merely that high-voltage AC lines may be more dangerous than anyone has realized. A new study made in Denver suggests that up to fifteen percent of the cases of childhood cancer in this country may be due to the electric and magnetic fields of high-voltage AC lines. If *that* is true, then the seventeen-times greater expense of burying power lines (if that power-company figure is correct) will come to look remarkably cheap.

Were the bolt weevils justified? To me, it seems they were. If a new power line equally dubious in origin were to come across my own farm, would I join a similar group? I don't know. I do know that I'd be tempted. And considering how much I dislike violence, how deeply I believe in a government of laws, not to mention how afraid I am of even traffic tickets, that's saying a lot.

[1989]

# War on the Farm

~

*Even while we talk some chemist at Columbia*
*Is stealthily contriving wool from jute*
*That when let loose upon the grazing world*
*Will put ten thousand farmers out of sheep.*

ROBERT FROST WROTE THOSE LINES in 1932. A lot more than
ten thousand farmers have been put out of sheep in the ensuing
fifty-nine years. Even those who still raise sheep do much better
selling Easter lambs than they do selling wool. I find with my own
handful of ewes that the cost of getting them sheared generally
exceeds the value of the fleece.

But things are even worse than Frost imagined. Having put
most sheep farmers out of business, the chemists went to work on
the jute farmers, and they have got some of them, too. When I
first bought a hundred pounds of feed for my first cow, it came in a
burlap sack — made, of course, of jute. Nice things, burlap sacks.
They had a dozen uses around the farm, such as storing fleeces
and holding apples en route to the cider mill. They were biode-
gradable besides.

Now when I buy a hundred pounds of grain, it comes in a
particularly nasty kind of woven plastic sack. Nasty (you mustn't,
for example, ever store a fleece in one — it contaminates the wool)
and practically immortal. Last summer I mowed a field for a
neighbor, a field he had once kept a couple of cows in and then let

go for several years. At some point back in his cow-keeping days he had left an empty plastic grain sack lying on the ground. When I mowed over it — it was hidden in weeds — it took me ten minutes to clear my cutter bar with pliers.

And then what to do with the pieces? I didn't dare burn them — God knows what I would have put in the atmosphere. In the end, I took them home in a paper bag to help fill up our town landfill.

Almost everything farmers do is threatened by technology. Often it's direct replacement. Artificial maple flavor for real, which will be particularly painful for Vermont, if the artificial flavor ever approaches the level of the real. Orlon socks instead of cotton. Synthetic "bacon bits." Every kind of Life Savers but two flavored with something made in a factory rather than grown on a farm.

Equally often, technology merely perverts true farming. People still raise chickens in order to get eggs — but those people are not exactly farmers anymore. And no child would recognize the places they operate as farms. Indeed, children are carefully kept away from modern 50,000-inmate chicken houses. Being young and innocent, they might think it was cruel to treat hens that way. They might even want to release them.

It can be argued, and often is, that all of these changes represent progress. Cheap food (eleven percent!) and cheap clothing are supplied by the chemists and the agrifactories, and if that means an end to traditional farming, well, times change.

Naturally I don't agree, and I'm not alone. The tremendous rise in demand for natural foods over the past ten years represents a horrified recoil by hundreds of thousands, perhaps even millions, of consumers. They have come to distrust not only junk food but the whole larger category of what I'm going to call tech food. They are thinking primarily about their own health (and their own taste buds), of course, but some of them also like the idea of supporting farms. Some of them deliberately seek out farmers' markets for that reason. And the resurgence of those markets is one of the few happy things that has happened recently. Ten years ago there were only nine in this state. Today there are eighteen.

But what about farmers themselves? What do they do to keep the grazing world (as Frost called it) alive? I see three common responses. And then there's a fourth one I don't often see but wish I did.

The most common response is to try to meet the factory on its own ground. Do you want to save your farm? Automate it. Reduce costs. If you're in the sheep business, for example, you might try to develop sheep-shearing robots so as to help keep the price of wool competitive with the price of polyester.

This is no fantasy. Australian farmers are in the process of developing such robots right now, just as Florida farmers, with assistance from the aerospace industry, are in the process of developing citrus-picking robots. *Big* farmers in Australia and Florida, that is. An expensive robot makes no sense at all if you have thirty sheep or one small grove of orange trees — but it might if you have six thousand sheep or a square mile of citrus.

It might. And in the long run, it might not too. If you fight technology with technology, technology fights back. The result is what used to be called a vicious circle and is now called escalation. The nuclear arms race is a familiar example.

Unfortunately for the farmer, when the Orlon factory gets its robots, it will be able to use them more efficiently than the sheep station, since it is dependent neither on the weather nor on the inherent one-at-a-time complexity of living creatures such as sheep. The chief result of robotizing sheep farms will be to reduce the number of shepherds still further, just as the chief result of Holsteinizing and milk-parlorizing dairy farms has been a drastic reduction in the number of dairy farmers. Drastic even in a stubbornly rural state like Vermont. Well over ten thousand Vermont dairy farmers have been put out of cows since Frost wrote his poem. There were 16,727 of them in 1932. There are 2,447 as I write. There will be fewer still when you read this.

A second response is to concede defeat on the main battle-ground and to look for little specialty markets that technology hasn't yet bothered with or can't at the moment handle. Take wool. I don't make any money on my fleeces, which are ordinary ones; but a small number of farmers produce special high-quality wool for the tiny hand-spinning market, and they get quite a decent price. Currently three or even five dollars a pound, versus the eighty-one cents (less fees) per pound that an ordinary fleece will bring through the Vermont Wool Pool.

Or consider maple sugar. It is never again going to have the role as a bulk sweetener that it once did, and even cane sugar is losing ground fast. Chemicals and corn syrup are what the Pepsi-Cola Company buys. But there remains a luxury market for maple sugar, and a health market both for it and for brown sugar. (Brown sugar may or may not be conducive to health, but there are lots of people who think it is.)

The third response, one possible only for part-time farmers, is to ignore or at least downplay the economic side of farming and to concentrate on its pleasures as a way of life. This way, you needn't compete with high-tech at all. If you want to shear your ewes with hand clippers just because it's an interesting thing to do, you are free to. Obviously you would have a very small flock, or it would cease to be an interesting thing to do. And while you'd still hope to sell the wool, the fact that your return for the time you put in breeding, raising, and shearing the sheep might come to thirty-six cents an hour simply doesn't matter. Your financial state is still better than that of the tennis player, whose return is something like minus six dollars an hour, or even the television viewer, at minus sixteen cents an hour.

I am this third kind of farmer myself, and I certainly don't mean to criticize play farms. I do hate the name, though. More accurately, they should be called owner-subsidized farms. We in the third class do plenty of hard work. It just happens to differ from most late-twentieth-century work in being deeply satisfying.

But what I have to note is that technology will eventually get most of us, too. Two of my own principal crops are maple syrup and firewood. I'll be able to go on making syrup for the luxury market (if acid rain doesn't kill my trees) even when the sophisticated process called reverse osmosis — which isn't economical on my small scale — has completely triumphed. I'll just make even less money per hour spent sugaring.

But when whole-tree chippers complete their triumph, and when states, pressed by the processed wood industry, begin to pass laws saying that the only legal woodstoves are those which burn wood chips, have fans, and theoretically pollute less, then where will the market be for my cut and split logs? Just about where the market for goose down will be when Thinsulate completes *its* triumph.

What we need is a fourth response: not turning the farm into a sort-of-factory, not settling for the economic crumbs left by technology, not pretending we're living fifty or a hundred years ago. We need to fight.

Farmers, of course, *do* fight — dumping milk, seeking quotas, trying to protect price supports. But mostly, they fight the wrong battles. Where we all should be fighting hardest is in the courts and in the newspapers, and what we should be attacking is the reckless use of technology. We should be trying to make the reckless users pay the true costs of what they do.

To what extent (if any) do artificial cherry and tangerine flavors turn Life Savers into life damagers? How many people have had allergic reactions to the synthetics used? I know one person who has, and she was rather sick. Are there others? A very few lawsuits might make it economical to use real cherry and tangerine flavors. What about the beef that gets imported from Central America? It is well known that when a dangerous pesticide or herbicide is banned in the United States, the companies that make it merely shift their markets overseas. DDT, for example, is freely sold in Central America and freely used in cattle ranching. I suspect we don't need a quota on beef; we merely need to make the chemical companies liable for any damage they do to human health in particular and to the health of the ecosystem in general. Organic beef might suddenly turn out to be a good buy.

What about plastic grain bags and, for that matter, polyester pants? If the true costs of dealing with the wastes put out by the factories that make these things are taken into account, not to mention the costs of getting rid of the sacks and the pants later, do burlap and wool remain more expensive?

What about those cheap broiler chickens raised on hormones? If it's the case, as it seems to be (it's not yet proved) that they play merry hell with the hormonal balance of some of the people who eat them — if the little girls who begin to menstruate at five years of age have been thus cruelly affected by eating too much biochemical chicken — then those chickens aren't really cheap at all. The health costs have merely been passed on to the public. If the producers had to assume these costs, then a decently raised farm chicken might turn out to be less expensive. These are some of the battles I'd like to see fought.

There is one caution I must add. It is easy to get paranoid on a subject like this, and it is easy (for me, anyway) to forget the many good things technology has done for farming and for human life in general. So let me grant that sometimes the new synthetic is better in every way than the old natural product. Let me further grant that the producers are not villains out to destroy rural life but just businessmen out to make money. And in the case of the scientists who make the actual discoveries, the motive isn't even money (usually) but pure, disinterested, irresponsible curiosity. As Frost says of science in the same poem I began with, it is something

Which for no sordid self-aggrandizement,
For nothing but its own blind satisfaction
(In this it is as much like hate as love)
Works in the dark as much against us as for us.

Blind? He's calling science and technology blind? Yes, he is —
often deliberately blind to the human consequences of the
changes they bring about. Far-sighted, of course, in many other
ways.

Science and technology do work for us. They also work against
us. All I'm saying is that in the latter cases, we'd better resist.
Otherwise, we may find ourselves with no farms, and eventually,
the human race may find itself with no habitable world.

[1986]

# ❧ VI ❧
# The (Partly) Happy Ending

# Tough Old Men

As I move into my late fifties, I begin to worry about what never concerned me before. Energy. My own personal energy, that is, not oil and gas. For thirty years I've been living in rural Vermont, and gradually inching nearer to being a farmer.

But can it last? I think I can sit on the tractor and mow indefinitely. But ten years from now, I wonder, will I still have the stamina to keep cutting and splitting wood for three stoves? Will I have the persistence to keep the fires going all winter? The moral fiber to step out into a sub-zero morning and feed the beef cattle? Or will I sensibly sell the cows? Go back to commercial heat? Will I eventually become one of those old codgers who slink off to Florida and hang around the shuffleboard court, waiting for spring?

Thoughts of two fellow New Englanders give me courage. One's a man named Brigham who raised apples in the next town. When I first met him, I was a mere child of forty — and him I took to be about the age I am now.

I'd gone to his place to buy apples. It was early December, and the hundred or so bushels he had left were down in the basement of his house. This you reached through a bulkhead and down a flight of stone steps. We were standing on those steps, talking. I'd selected my bushel — good Winesaps — and he was holding them in a wooden apple box, which he rested on one knee as we talked.

We were discussing a mutual friend, another orchardist named Augustus Aldrich. I had lately been to see Mr. Aldrich, one of whose great-nephews was a student of mine. In fact I had worked most of the day in his cider mill.

"You know," I said, "the amazing thing is that he runs that farm all by himself — well, maybe a little help from his nephew and great-nephews — and he's eighty-one years old."

Mr. Brigham, still holding my bushel of Winesaps against his knee, gave me a long slow look. "What's so damn special about that?" he asked. "I'm eighty-three."

The other man I met even longer ago, when I was a downright infant of perhaps thirty-two. I'd gone to a church supper, here in our own village. It was the kind where you sit at long tables, and each table gets filled up before anyone may go start a fresh one. I thus found myself sitting next to a stranger, a white-haired man with one leg in a cast and a pair of crutches leaning on the wall behind him. At thirty-two I was not a good judge of age — over sixty they all looked the same to me. But this man was clearly *old*. He had wrinkles, liver spots, what I must regretfully call wattles. He did seem reasonably muscular.

We got to talking over the chicken pot pie. He was from a village about ten miles away, and being bored with his leg in a cast, was going to all the church suppers in the region.

"How did you break your leg?" I asked, not because I particularly cared (over sixty it must happen all the time), but because it's the sort of question one is supposed to ask.

He didn't get a chance to answer. His wife, a large white-haired woman in the seat beyond him, had clearly been listening to our conversation. Now she leaned toward me. "The old fool fell off the roof," she said.

He had no snappy answer for this unillusioned wifely remark. His jaw opened and shut once or twice. Then he spoke, almost apologetically. "You didn't like the roof leaking any better'n me. *Someone* had to fix it."

That's what I hope to be in another twenty years: an old fool up on the roof. It may just be that the never-ending work of a hill farm keeps people — not young, nothing does that — but tough to the end.

[1986]

POSTSCRIPT: It seems to be working. Too soon to say for sure, because Floyd and I aren't old enough yet. But we're getting near. He is seventy-eight, and I'm over sixty. Last year, he was in bad shape, and unable to do more than a very little haying. But this year! This year he got the entire village baled before the end of June, which is the earliest he has ever done it.

Partly this was the result of exceptionally good haying weather — it has been exceptionally good weather for everything. Back in March and April we got exactly the right combination of freezing nights and warm days for maple sugaring, and most of us made more syrup than we have in at least five years. In May we had exactly the right weather for bees to pollinate fruit trees, and it looks like it will be a record apple, plum, and cherry year. Strawberry season came two weeks early, and has been terrific. I've seldom seen so much fruit on the black raspberry bushes.

But it wasn't just the good weather that enabled Floyd to finish so fast. He has seemed tireless. Usually he has one grandson or another to help at haying time, but it happened that none were free this year. So Floyd has moved from hayfield to hayfield alone — mowing, tedding, raking, baling. He did get some help from people in the village in picking up the bales and putting them in the barn; that tradition continues.

But even with bale-lifters to help, haying is a lot of work. There are many days when Floyd was out in the field from the time the dew dried off until the sun set — say, ten A.M. until eight P.M. And don't think he was lolling around until ten. He feels so much better he has bought a new milk cow, and of course he has his usual thirty or so sheep to look after.

As for me, I've done a little mowing, too. Floyd, of course, came over to ted and rake the hay for me. He did let me do some of the baling, which takes less skill. I've also been putting up a new horse fence at my wife's farm, and a new woodshed here. I even spent several hours padding around the roof, getting the boards up and driving the nails, and managed not to fall off. Naturally. That experience I'm not ready for yet. I'm still too young.

[1991]

# My Farm Is Safe Forever

❧

EVERY DAY THERE ARE NINETY-THREE fewer farms in America than there were the day before. Some get amalgamated into agri-business holdings, and a few are simply abandoned. Most, how-ever, get paved, built on, developed, or occasionally turned into nature preserves.

None of these fates awaits my farm. It's going to stay a farm long after I have moved into the village cemetery. Long after my grandchildren — and I don't even have any yet — have done the same. In fact, forever. And if that seems too huge a claim, just wait a minute.

I can speak with such confidence for an excellent reason. A few years ago I made a solemn and binding agreement with the small Vermont town I live in. I gave the town the development rights to my farm. For its part, the town agreed never to use them. If the town ever changes its mind — if, say a hundred years from now, whoever is running things gets tired of holding the rights — they automatically pass to a private conservation group three towns away. Should that no longer be around, the development rights go to its successor organization.

Meanwhile, I still own the place. I still possess every right of ownership that I care about. I can continue to raise beef cattle, bale hay, make maple syrup, cut logs, make whatever rural use of my ninety acres I feel like. If that begins to bore me (it won't), I can sell to any buyer I please. I could even sell the place to

189

McDonald's. It's just that if they bought it, they couldn't put up any golden arches. They'd have to install a farm manager, and start raising beef cattle, making maple syrup, or whatever.

I gave up the right to develop my farm solely to protect the land, but as a kind of bonus there are some pleasant cash benefits. Getting rid of the development rights has assured lower taxes on the place, for me and for all future owners.

The taxes will stay exactly the same on the house and on the two acres around it — what our state government calls a homestead. But on the other eighty-eight there will be a highly pleasing difference. From now on, these eighty-eight acres — my present fields and woods — will be taxed on their value as farmland and woodlot, not on what they might be worth if they were converted into forty-four building lots, or a tennis club. (That forty-four is not random. It's the maximum number of lots a developer could impose on my farm: we have two-acre rural zoning in this part of town. Actually, what with the roads the developer would have to put in and the steepness of a couple of my hills, I suspect he or she would have to scramble to put in more than about thirty-five new houses. That's still thirty-five more than I want.)

Back to the money. As I was saying, the taxes are now lower. But that's not all. The difference between my place's value as a farm and its value as developable land, which the town listers worked out to be $27,800, counted as a charitable deduction on my income tax. Need I say I've never had a deduction like that before? Since my income was nowhere near high enough to use it all in one year (still isn't), I had a carryover deduction for the next year — and there was still some left for the year after that. Most fun I've ever had with the IRS, or ever expect to have.

This was no slick private deal, either. It was not arranged or suggested by a tax lawyer. It is something almost any farmer can do. In fact, you don't even have to be a farmer. You just have to be the owner of a fair-sized piece of open land that qualifies under "a clearly defined federal, state or local government conservation policy." I'm quoting IRS Publication 526, entitled "Charitable Contributions," the same lovely document that enables me to talk so grandly about permanence. The tax benefits apply, says Publication 526, only if the land is "protected forever." Suits me. Even though I secretly know that "forever" means something like "as long as the United States exists in its present form." That's likely to be a while.

The luck is that such laws exist. It took more than luck, however, to get my farm protected under them. It took persistence, a good bit of paperwork — and, of course, the willingness to give up the profits I might have made by selling to a developer.

I first began thinking about protecting the farm in the spring of 1980. Two things set me going. One was the particularly brutal fate of a farm a few miles away, a dairy farm that had been in the same family for more than a hundred years. That place wasn't developed; it was dismembered. It had been my idea of a perfect farm.

The other was that my children were growing up. I have two, both girls. The older, having lived in rural Vermont all her life, was talking longingly about London. The younger was beginning to dream of being an airline flight attendant. It seemed clear to them that they didn't want to be farmers or farmers' wives, or country dwellers at all. It seemed clear to me that when I died the natural thing would be for them to sell the place. Having spent twenty years restoring it to a beautiful and moderately productive farm, I didn't relish the idea of bulldozers leveling my carefully rebuilt stone walls or blacktoppers advancing into the orchard.

The first step was a serious discussion with my daughters. I began with a little lecture on what it means to own a piece of land. Not what it means emotionally (they've known all about that since they were little), but what it means legally. To own a piece of land, I explained to two moderately bored teenagers, is to own a bundle of rights, most of which can be separated from each other. For example, you can detach the mineral rights from a piece of land and sell them, while still keeping the land itself. You can also detach the right to develop, and lock it safely away. That was what I wanted to do. If I did, it would mean my daughters would inherit something considerably reduced in value. Reduced $27,800, to be precise, though of course I didn't have that figure then. It would be even more now.

In some ways Americans are the least materialistic of all people. The girls didn't hesitate a second. "Dad, we know how you love the place," my elder daughter said. "We love it, too. We just don't want to spend our lives looking after cows. You go right ahead."

Despite their encouragement, I didn't do anything more for about a year and a half. Partly that was to give the girls a chance to change their minds. Mostly it's just the way I operate. Slowly. I'm the sort of person who can decide he needs a tractor and then spend several years thinking about it before actually going out and buying one. During the next eighteen months I collected a fat folder of clippings about development rights, but that was all I did.

Then in the fall of 1981 I finally made a move — in fact, a double move. We have a planning commission in our town, and I wrote its chairperson to ask if the town would be interested in a gift of development rights. And I put the same question to what was then the Ottauquechee Regional Land Trust and has since tripled in size and become the Vermont Land Trust. At the time, it was the nearest to me of the many hundreds of land trusts that have sprung up across America in the last ten or fifteen years. (There are also some, mostly in the Northeast, that have been around much longer.) I knew about Ottauquechee from my clipping file.

Not surprisingly, the planning commission replied cautiously, since no one had ever made such an offer to the town before. They said come to a meeting and tell them about it, which I did. Then they deliberated for three months. Then they decided to pass my query on to the selectmen. (For those who don't follow the minutiae of New England customs, selectmen are what we have as local government, rather than mayors and councils, county commissioners, and the like. Some towns have five selectmen, some three. This one has three.)

Also not surprisingly, the Ottauquechee Land Trust replied with a good deal more zest. Though only four years old at the time, it had lots of experience with development rights, and at that moment was working on roughly a dozen cases. Richard Carbin, the vigorous young director, first wrote me, then phoned, then came over and walked the farm with me. That was to make sure it really could function agriculturally into the indefinite future. On a small scale, it can. I've got two or three nice pastures. Any time I was ready to protect them, he said, the trust was ready to cooperate.

Meanwhile, the selectmen had also been thinking. Their decision was that something like this had better come up at Town Meeting. If the voters approved, they wouldn't oppose the gift. If the voters turned it down, naturally that ended the matter.

Furthermore, instead of placing my offer on the agenda themselves, the selectmen felt I should do it by petition. That's work. Such a petition must be signed by five percent of the voters in town, which at that time was sixty-five people. (It's currently seventy-four.) Getting up a petition is not difficult or technical — every year we have two or three articles to discuss at Town Meeting that have been petitioned by individuals rather than warned by the selectmen — but it does take a little time and effort.

By now we were well into 1982. I had a choice to make. I could quickly donate rights to the land trust. Or more slowly, and with some bother, I could give them to the town.

I chose to go the town route, and I had three reasons. One was emotional. I like the direct democracy of Town Meeting, and I liked the idea of the voters' making the decision. One of the ways we educate ourselves in rural New England is by arguing things out at Town Meeting.

The second reason was practical and involved taxes. The big

question for both the planning board and the selectmen had been precisely how much real estate tax the town would lose if my farm ceased to be developable. Towns hate losing revenue. The question was complicated, because my thirty-two acres of pasture, though not the fifty-six acres of woodland, were already enrolled in a state program of current-use taxation. The town taxed part of the place as farmland, the rest as potential development land, and the state made up the difference. All of us assumed the state contribution would cease once I gave away the development rights. Our best guess was that the town would lose about $400 a year if the gift went through.

Of course I could have thumbed my nose at the selectmen and gone straight to the land trust — but only at the cost of enraging some of my neighbors and maybe giving conservation a bad name locally for years to come. If my taxes went down, wouldn't everybody else's have to go up, however slightly? Wouldn't it in fact look like a slick private deal? I preferred to face people at Town Meeting and so get a chance to make the case that in the long run land protection holds down everybody's taxes.

That's where the clipping file would come in handy. I thought the story of Suffolk County, Long Island, for example, might catch people's attention. I had a clipping that said the county authorities there had raised a sum of $60 million to *buy* development rights on farmland. They figured on protecting twelve thousand acres at a cost of $5,000 an acre. And then they expected to recoup that whole enormous sum "in terms of tax dollars that won't have to be spent on more schools, roads, and services." If purchased rights pay for themselves, what a bargain free ones must be.

I had another good clipping, too — this one about a county in Virginia that did a close study of where it got its money and where it then spent it. Turned out that for every tax dollar the county took in from farmland and woodland, it only had to spend about seventy cents. But for every dollar it got from developed land, it spent \$1.11. It made sense to me. Cows don't go to school. And counties don't have to maintain farm roads.

Finally, I had a personal financial reason for donating my development rights to the town rather than the land trust. Land trusts need revenue just as much as towns do. They've got to have offices, phones, files, legal advice, the lot. The older ones have depended on the traditional income sources of nonprofit organizations: membership dues and fund drives. Many also keep their expenses down by hiring no paid staff whatsoever. In Connecticut, a pioneering state in land conservation, there are eighty-two small land trusts, almost double the number in any other state. According to Allan Spader, director of the recently formed Land Trust Exchange in Boston, all but two or three depend entirely on volunteer staff.

But some of the newer land trusts, with much to do and little time to do it in, are experimenting with a sort of fee-for-service approach. The donor of development rights is asked also to make a cash contribution which will become endowment for the trust. Montana Land Alliance uses that approach and so, as it happens, does the Vermont Land Trust. It asks for three percent of the value of the land to be protected.

That seems perfectly reasonable. We who donate the land get tax savings much larger than three percent of the value of the land. The trust has an urgent need for money. Fund drives are more difficult to conduct in a poor state like Vermont than in a rich state like Connecticut. All that I see. But I have the misfortune to be a born tightwad. If I could save the three percent, I still preferred to. I began to prepare for the 1983 Town Meeting.

Getting the signatures for my petition proved to be extremely easy. I had been dreading it, because I hate going house to house asking for something, even if it's only signatures. Then the woman who runs the store in our village made a good suggestion. I wrote a brief account of what I wanted to do, stapled it to a sheet of blank paper, and left it on the store counter.

Within a week I had almost fifty signatures. When a second week produced only three more, I made a copy of my statement, and with the owner's consent left that on the counter of the general store in one of the other villages in town. Quite soon I was up to sixty-seven signatures, two more than needed. When the warning for Town Meeting was posted on January 24, 1983, Article XI read, "To see if the Town wishes to accept a gift of the development rights to Noel Perrin's farm in Thetford Center."

Before Town Meeting we have an event called Pre–Town Meeting. It comes a week ahead. All the candidates for office attend; so do people who have a petitioned article, and usually about fifty or so of the more serious voters. There is time to go into issues more deeply than is sometimes possible at Town Meeting itself.

My proposal got a cool reception. No one actually said "slick private deal," but clearly the people who asked me questions were thinking about the lost $400. Someone mused out loud on what would happen if other landowners began doing the same thing — what would happen to his own taxes, that is. Naturally I had my clipping with me. But he and the other questioners were not much impressed by the news from Suffolk County, Long Island, or even by what was happening much nearer at hand in Massachusetts. *That's them; we're us*, seemed to be the feeling.

I went home depressed. It didn't cheer me a bit when the chairman of our Board of Selectmen (I've known her for twenty years) called me that evening. "I'm going to move to pass over your article," Ginny said. "You'll do better to wait a year. It doesn't stand a chance now."

People who work for land trusts are generally idealists. I had stayed in touch with Rick Carbin at Ottauquechee all this time. (I had also become a dues-paying member of the trust. Still am.) He wasn't in the least touchy that I was going the town route; what mattered was protecting another farm.

The next morning I phoned him for advice. Don't even consider giving up, he said. Instead, quickly get in touch with the town clerk of Pomfret, Vermont. She can tell you something that will interest the voters in your town.

The result was that when I went to Town Meeting, I not only had with me a list of facts and figures, such as that we had lost 153 farms in Orange County, Vermont, in the preceding ten years, I had a brief letter from Hazel Harrington, the town clerk of Pomfret. That was my secret weapon. Only the head selectman knew about it. It had persuaded her not to pass over Article XI, after all.

When it came my turn, I made a brief but passionate speech. Just to warm up, I mentioned Long Island, Massachusetts, and the lost 153 farms in our own county. Then I brought out the secret weapon. I told the meeting there was one precedent for what I proposed to do. In 1981, Henry Bourne of Pomfret had deeded development rights on a piece of land to his town, the first person in the state to make that kind of gift. Then I read Mrs. Harrington's letter.

> Dear Mr. Perrin,
>
> The land on which Mr. Bourne deeded development right to the Town of Pomfret is listed no different for tax purposes than it was before he took this action. He retained title to the property. However, he as an individual is in the current-use program. Therefore, the Town is getting the same amount of taxes on this property as before.

Thetford Town Meeting took that in. Then it heard me promise to get my woodlot into the current-use program, along with the pastures. Then a couple of people asked perfunctory questions. Then the town voted overwhelmingly to accept my offer, and we went on to Article XII.

And that's how my farm comes to be safe, if not forever, at least for a long time to come. That's how I came to have a $27,800 income-tax deduction for doing what I wanted to do anyway. If you are a landowner, you, too, can probably make money by protecting your land. Ecologically, aesthetically, and morally, that seems preferable to the traditional practice of making money by destroying it.

[1984]

POSTSCRIPT: It's now eight years since that town meeting. Thetford is under a lot more development pressure than it was in 1983. It is also much more used to the idea that when developers push one way, it is perfectly all right to push back the other way. We now have a town Conservation Commission, which played a key role in saving Earl LaMountain's farm last year. That's a full working farm, as opposed to my half-working farm.

Its members were also busy two years ago, when the old Shyott place got sold to a developer. The sale was not stopped, nor am I sure it should have been. There are three million more Americans every year, all needing a place to live. Lots of them want to live in the country, and Thetford will get its share, as it got me, thirty years ago. The good news is that part of the Shyott place will stay country for them to live in. The big twelve-acre hayfield at the front will stay a hayfield, and the handful of new houses will be up behind, well spread out. Under pressure, the developers themselves put on conservation restrictions.

The Conservation Commission didn't bring that about all by itself. We also have a new and even closer-to-hand land trust. I belong to that one, too. The Upper Valley Land Trust was the other key player in saving LaMountain's farm and keeping a rural aspect to Shyott.

What about my own farm? That hasn't changed a bit, except that I finally ditched the upper meadow, and I've put up one new stone wall. My older daughter did get to London but came home after two years. She now lives in Seattle. The younger one is in Boston. Taxes continue to climb, of course. It's no longer $400 a year that I save by having conservation restrictions on the place;

last year it was $817.03. The town got reimbursed by the state, same as always.

What if one day the state gives up its current-use program, and therefore quits reimbursing towns? That would certainly be a blow. A minor blow. The taxes of everyone in town, me included, would go up an average of sixty cents.

On the other hand, suppose I had sold out eight years ago. Suppose there were now thirty-five houses on what used to be my farm. In *that* case, everybody's taxes would have gone up somewhere between $100 and $500. I still think the town got a bargain. And so did I.

[1991]

NOEL PERRIN, teacher, writer, and farmer (in that order) is a professor of Environmental Studies at Dartmouth College. He and his wife, the novelist Anne Lindbergh, live partly on his farm in Thetford, Vermont, and partly on hers in Barnet. His articles and reviews have appeared in *Country Journal*, *Vermont Life*, *The New Yorker*, *New England Monthly*, and many other publications. His books include *Giving Up the Gun: Japan's Reversion to the Sword, 1543–1879*; *Dr. Bowdler's Legacy: A History of Expurgated Books*; and *First, Second,* and *Third Person(s) Rural*, all published by Godine.

Last Person Rural

has been set on the Linotron 202 in Janson, an old style face first
issued by Anton Janson in Leipsic between 1660 and 1687, and
typical of the Low Country designs broadly disseminated throughout
Europe and the British Isles during the seventeenth century. The
contemporary versions of this eminently readable and widely employed typeface are based upon type cast from the original matrices,
now in the possession of the Stempel Type Foundry
in Frankfurt, Germany.